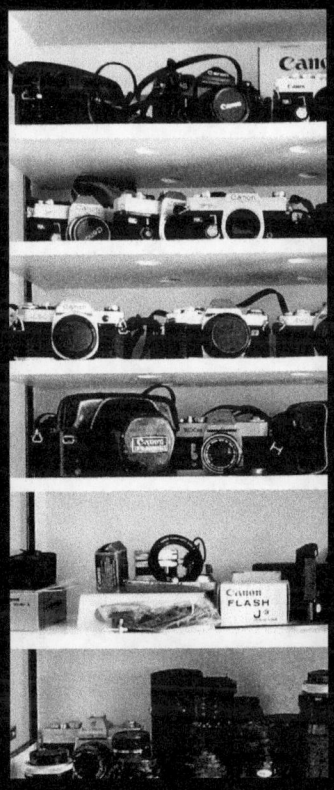
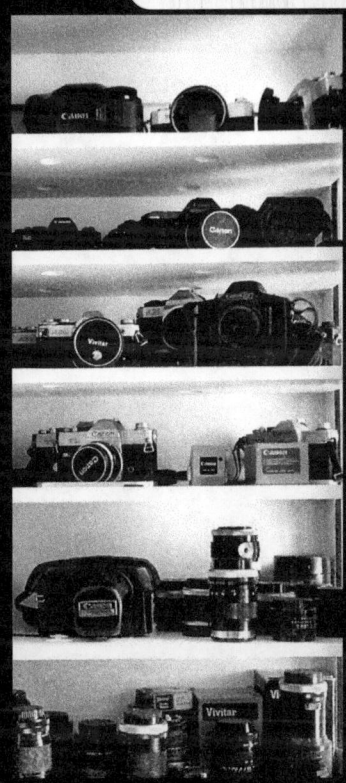

Canon Manual Focus SLRs
A Collectors' Guide

Eric Skopec, Ph. D.

Canon Manual Focus SLRs/A Collectors' Guide

©Eric Skopec 2011

All Rights Reserved

ISBN: 978-1463674687

Acknowledgements

I was just beginning to understand photography when I wandered into Terry's Cameras in Long Beach, California. The display windows were well stocked with modern and classic gear, and I soon learned that Terry's was one of the premier camera shops in Southern California.

Over the next several years, the owner Maurice Greeson and his senior floor person Leigh St. Maur Stocker spent countless hours educating me. Maurice is a walking encyclopedia on photographic processes and equipment while Leigh was an occasionally gruff but always insightful critic.

Terry's and Leigh are both gone now, victims of urban renewal and a life well lived, respectively. Maurice is happily retired in Utah and found time to review much of this manuscript. He tracked down brand details for many of the third-party lenses described in Chapter 5.

Members of the Kiron Klub added many details to the same chapter and saved me from publishing potentially embarassing errors. Members of the Camera_Fix group contributed many of the ideas on inspection and cleaning. Members of the FD Users Group and the FD Forum also contributed a great deal and helped to keep my toes from the fire. Special thanks go to Carl Follstad, Zheng (James) Peng, Gordon Yee, and Mark Wahlster.

Advance readers included Robert W. Bowman, Jr., Hans de Groot, Ed Lutz, Louis Lung, and Chuck Norcutt. They found innumerable errors and I am gratful for their careful attention.

Finally, this project builds on the legacy of earlier writers. Bob Shell's *Canon Compendium*, Peter Dechert's *Canon Single Lens Reflex Lens Cameras/1959-1991*, McKeowns' *Price Guide to Antique and Classic Cameras*, McBroom's *Camera Bluebook*, and Christian Rollinger's Canon FD Documentation Project all merit special commendation.

Thank you all. You've added incomparable pleasure to my collecting activities and established a solid foundation on which this small book builds.

Preface

This small book began with my efforts to make sense out of my collection of Canon manual focus bodies, lenses, and accessories. As the collection expanded, so did my reading. I digested the standard works mentioned in the Acknowledgements and then discovered the wealth of information available on the Internet. At the same time, I acquired a small set of "classic" works including Curtin & London's *The Canon Camera Handbook,* Emanuel's *Canon Reflex Guide,* Francke's *Canon Modern Classics,* Shell and Francke's *Canon Classic Cameras,* and Shipman's *Canon SLR Cameras.* I also rediscovered the wealth of information in original instruction sheets and product guides.

Remarkably, or so it seemed to me, the various accounts are not always consistent. Many of the inconsistencies have spawned lively online discussions and invited informed commentaries. As I tried to sort out the various opinions, I began to collect articles, citations, and comments in a small notebook dedicated to that purpose. Eventually, the small notebook grew to three large binders plus several gigabytes of computer files.

On a rainy afternoon, I realized that I had the makings of a small book that might interest collectors and users. I set out to organize the various clippings, articles, and other ephemera into a comprehensive collector's guide. I hoped to help readers place their cherished items in an historical context; recognize uniquely valuable bodies, lenses, and accessories; distinguish between collectible, usable, repairable, and irretrievably damaged pieces; identify cult classic lenses that are easy to overlook, and display their collections to best advantage.

I suspect I have fallen short in some respects. Chapter 4 dealing with accessories was particularly difficult owing to the lack of reliable documentation. Fortunately, my publisher makes it possible to produce new editions relatively quickly. If you find errors or omissions, please email me at ewskopec@yahoo.com and I will revise the text accordingly.

Contents

Introduction

Collecting classic cameras, lenses, and accessories is a remarkably engaging hobby. Some people might even call it an obsession.

A few people do it for profit—buying, repairing, and reselling classic cameras. Most collectors have other motives. Some enjoy the solid feel and visual impact of the cameras. Many enjoy researching the cameras' histories while searching for specific models entertains other collectors. Some even enjoying owning cameras that were beyond their means when they were younger. Personally, I enjoy all of the above as well as capturing stunning images with my classics.

Other authors have said more about the joys of collecting. I won't repeat their remarks because I doubt that you would have opened this book if you weren't already interested. Instead, I'll begin with six important precepts.

First, collections come in all sizes and shapes.

There is no single correct approach to collecting. Some private collections have hundreds or even thousands of items; others have just a few selected bodies and lenses. Many collections contain artifacts manufactured by specific companies or produced in distinct periods while others include anything that interests the collector.

Many collections have only bodies and lenses. Others include winders, flashes, finders, macro accessories, users manuals, sales literature, display stands and third party books. Some even include advertisements and promotional materials as well as clocks, ashtrays, watches and cigarette lighters.

Some collections reside in humidity controlled display cases; others line shelves, nestle in drawers and cabinets, fill cardboard boxes or rest on work benches. My collection is somewhere in the middle; when my display cabinets overflow, additional items go where ever there is space. Not even the china cabinet in our dining room is exempt—much to my wife's chagrin.

The important point is that collecting is a very personal activity. Collections reflect the interests, resources, and abilities of the collectors. The act of collecting preserves important bits of photographic history and provides very real pleasure for the collectors.

Second, condition like beauty is in the eye of the beholder.

Few 50-year old cameras, lenses, and accessories survive in pristine condition. Some have been bashed, broken, and abused, but most have modest scratches, abrasions, and other defects. Some collectors turn their noses up at obviously well used items, but I see the imperfections are part of the camera's life story.

Collectors and dealers use grading schemes to note imperfections and describe the items in their collections. A widely recognized scheme used by *Shutterbug* grades cameras on a scale from "mint" to "ugly" with five intermediate grades.[1] Buy an "excellent" camera from a reputable dealer using the scheme and you should receive a camera with 80 to 89% of its original finish as well as perfect optics and flawless mechanics.

Unfortunately, even the most honest dealers may inadvertently overlook flaws. Problems increase as you move down the grading scale. Boundaries between lower grades can be fuzzy and less scrupulous sellers may inflate the condition of their goods. Worse yet, some sellers invent their own categories or add adjectives to minimize imperfections. "Spectacular," "gorgeous," "beautiful," "minty," "like new minus," and "nearly excellent" often say more about the sellers than the cameras.[2]

Third, cameras, lenses, and other collectibles are worth exactly what someone is willing to pay for them—no more, no less![3]

Economists think of prices in terms of supply, demand, and disparities in available information. That's well and good if you are fond of theories, but a glance at camera prices on eBay is just as informative. Recent prices for Canon AE-1s, for example, have ranged from under $20 to over $98 for cameras in roughly comparable condition! Pricing is even more complicated for "kits," "sets" and "outfits." For example, one EBay seller recently listed a "beautiful AE-1 kit" with three lenses, light meter, leather

1 The Appendix summarizes some common grading schemes.
2 Chapter 6 suggests some strategies for protecting yourself.
3 Published guides like the McKeowns' *Price Guide to Antique and Classic Cameras* suggest price ranges based on average recent selling prices at selected auctions.

case, filters, and accessories. The asking price was $400, but savvy buyers could create the same kit for just under $90 by buying the items separately. Moreover, market conditions can change rapidly--from week to week or even day to day. "Hot" items selling for $200 one week may sell for around $35 or less the following week. It all depends on who is buying, what they want, and how much they are prepared to pay.

Fourth, prices are not entirely random.

Variability does not mean that prices are entirely random. Experienced collectors base their pricing decisions on five considerations:

1. Historical Significance. Cameras that introduced new functions and feature sets are historically significant and typically command higher prices than "run of the mill" cameras. For example, Canon's first professional SLR, the F1, generally sells for more than twice as much as other Canons of the era. The third and final version of the F1 (the "New F1") was an extraordinarily capable camera for its era and typically sells for three times as much as the original F1.

2. Original Quality. Leica cameras are valuable because people appreciate their quality. Similarly, Canon's L class lenses are several times more valuable than their common siblings. Likewise, T70 bodies are more highly valued than the T60 because they are better built.

3. Rarity. Some cameras had short production runs and relatively few are available. In general, rare cameras command higher prices than more common models. For example, collectors pay more for Canonflex models than for more functional FXs or FTbs. Similarly, the meterless FP commands higher prices than the FX on which its based and the FDn 50mmf2 lens is considered more collectable than the substantially better FDn 50mmf1.8.[4]

4. Condition. Even cameras that have been worn and abused may retain some value if they are rare or historically significant. However, other things being equal, cameras, lenses, and accessories in Mint condi-

---

4 Coincidentally, interests of collectors and users diverge on this criterion. Some cameras are rare because they were commercial flops and relatively few were produced. This appeals to collector, but users may be happier with a common AE-1 than a Canonflex.

tion are more valuable than those in Excellent or lower grade condition. Values fall rapidly as condition deteriorates and inoperative pieces may have little value unless some other feature makes them desirable.

5. Personal Interest. Collectors may pay more than expected for items that appeal to them for other reasons. A camera from a family members' estate may interest them as do cameras popular during their childhoods. Similarly, they may need a particular piece to complete a portion of their collection and be willing to pay far more than other factors would indicate. Even off-beat, cheaply made cameras can command high prices if they appeal to the personal interests of a handful of collectors.

Fifth, knowledge of cameras and photography is the foundation of camera collecting.

Simply holding a classic camera can be a pleasure and the joy is magnified when you know when and where the camera was produced. Enthusiasm grows as you learn why the camera is historically significant and what lenses or accessories complement it to produce a complete photographer's kit.

Collectors learn by buying, testing, and comparing cameras, lenses and accessories. They also learn by talking to dealers and other collectors, participating in users groups, researching specific models, and reading users' manuals, books, articles, and web pages. Learning is a continuous process and it generally shows up in three features of a collection.

1. Knowing about cameras and photography helps you to define your collection and select individual pieces that fit in. You might concentrate on items by particular companies or specific types of camera. My own collection is defined by manufacturer and type (Canon Manual Focus SLRs). Other possibilities include time periods, particular innovations or historically significant cameras, variations on particular models, family traditions, and even cameras used by selected—generally famous—photographers.

2. Learning about cameras also helps to organize and display your collection. With a general plan, its easy to place individual items and explain why they are important. Visitors can see everything in context and you can add interesting details when visitors ask. Cameras in my display cases are arranged in chronological order and its easy for me to explain the features and functions that each model added to the line up.

3. Collateral material is an important part of every collection. Few used cameras come with all the original literature, but you can find much of it on the Internet. Users' manuals and product guides have pride of place in my displays, but I also keep warranty cards, boxes and packing materials, classic reviews, and third-party books. I frame some advertisements as wall displays and keep a notebook of reproduced users manuals, reviews, articles and other things that help me understand the artifacts on display.[5]

Finally, every collector makes a few mistakes.

Canon manual focus SLRs, lenses, and accessories are generally well marked and counterfeiting is yet to become problematic.[6] However recognizing variations within models requires some background. For example, Canon made six distinct manual focus lenses of 35mm. Some are highly desirable while others are just usable consumer grade lenses. Similarly, Canon made changes in bodies without adding identifying marks. For example, there are three F-1s,[7] two FTbs, and two EFs.

There are even more opportunities for confusion when purchasing lenses and accessories by third-party manufacturers. For example, Vivitar contracted with a variety of manufacturers and the quality of their lenses is uneven.[8] Lenses produced by Kiron are very desirable and command

---

5 The Bibliography lists some places where you can download collateral materials.

6 Black or professional bodies are an exception to the statement that counterfeiting is not a problem. In recent months, user groups have fielded questions from people seeking ways to repaint chrome models and increase their perceived values.

7 Or four if you count unmodified variations of the first model. Initial production models could not mount the motor drive unit and Canon modified them at no cost if owners requested the service.

8 See Chapter 5 for Vivitar serial numbers and manufacturers.

premium prices. Many, but not all, made by other suppliers are marginal performers, at best, and regularly sell for $15 to $25.

With knowledge and experience, you will learn to distinguish variations in the bodies, lenses, and accessories, but it takes time. Moreover, it takes a fine eye to recognize some defects and distinguish between repairable items and those destined for second lives as paper weights.

While you learn, there are predictable errors. Novice collectors typically pay too much for commonplace items, offer too little for highly desirable pieces, and buy unrepairable items. Don't feel bad when you fall victim to one of these common errors, but do learn from the experience. If it helps, you can think of the costs incurred as the price of a first-class education.

What's ahead?

The six precepts above provide a solid foundation for collecting cameras, lenses, and accessories. Applying them to Canon manual focus SLRs requires some background. This book aims to provide information that will make your hobby more enjoyable and avoid some common errors.

Much of the information is available elsewhere. You could gather it from books, user manuals and assorted Internet pages as I have done. At the very least, this book will save you hours of research.

Other bits of information are less durable. They are stored in the memories of "old timers," people who were working professionals when the cameras were new. I've corresponded with many, but the number dwindles every day.

This book is organized to make it easy for you to find the information you need. Chapter 1 is a brief history of Canon and the company's manual focus SLRs and Chapter 2 lists the cameras along with important details about each.

Chapter 3 describes the four generations of Canon manual focus SLR lenses. They are designated by letters corresponding to camera mounts: R (1959-1963), FL (1964-1971), FD (1971-1978), and FDn or "new FD" (1978-1994).

Canon manual focus SLRs were the centerpieces of comprehensive camera systems. Power winders, flashes, focusing screens, finders and other accessories outfitted the cameras to serve a variety of purposes. Chapter 4 describes the most important Canon accessories and identifies the bodies with which each can be used.

Chapter 5 describes some of the more interesting third party lenses for Canon manual focus SLRs. Some companies produced outstanding lenses while other firms sold barely adequate lenses for cost conscious consumers. This chapter tells a bit of the Vivitar story, identifies some "cult classic" lenses, and identifies over 80 other third-party lens manufacturers and distributors.

Chapter 6 outlines some approaches to managing your collection. It covers finding, inspecting, buying, recording, cleaning and displaying classic cameras along with some other important concerns.

The Appendix picks up three important themes briefly mentioned in the text. It summarizes common grading schemes and their limitations as well as procedures for inspecting and cleaning photographic equipment.

The Bibliography lists additional sources you may wish to consult.

Chapter 1: Canon Manual Focus SLRs in Perspective

Today, Canon, Inc. is a world-leading optics company. Over the last decade, Canon has consistently earned more patents than any other company except IBM. Canon products include office equipment, digital printing presses, medical imaging systems, software, and commercial broadcasting equipment.

For all this variety, Canon is first and foremost a camera company. The company began by manufacturing 35mm cameras and its growth tracks changes in the photographic industry. Much of its story can be told in terms of three generations of camera systems.

Figure 1.1: Canon Cameras in perspective

1930s	1940s	1950s	1960s	1970s	1980s	1990s
	Rangefinder Era					
			Manual Focus SLR Era			
						EOS Era . . . .

The Rangefinder Era

Canon traces its origin to the Precision Optical Instruments Laboratory. Founded in Tokyo in 1933, the company began by producing Leica-like rangefinder cameras. The founders[1] produced their first prototype, the Kwanon, in 1934 and began marketing production models of the Hansa Canon in 1936.

In spite of improvements, all prewar models displayed their German heritage. The Second World War retarded further development, but Canon resumed production around 1946. It appears that many early postwar units were hand made from left over parts.

American occupation of Japan opened a new market for Canon. Many returning US service personnel brought cameras home with them. The process continued during the Korean war because Japan was the primary staging area for United Nations troops. Cameras sold in post exchanges are marked <EP> and countless service personnel brought them home as souvenirs.

---

1 Takeshi Mitarai, Goro Yoshida, Saburo Uchida and Takeo Maeda.

The US Market was so promising that Canon established distribution agreements with two American companies. In 1950, the C. R. Skinner Company in San Francisco became the first factory-authorized importer of Canon cameras. Cameras imported by skinner have engraved baseplates noting that they were "MADE IN OCCUPIED JAPAN/SERVICED AND GUARANTEED IN SAN FRANCISCO CALIFORNIA."

A decade later, Canon entered into a distribution agreement with Bell & Howell. Although Canon opened its own New York office in 1955, the agreement with Bell & Howell continued in force through the early 1970s. Many bodies carry the Bell & Howell name, while some have only the Canon name, and a few have both names.

Figure 1.2 Bell & Howell Auto 35/Reflex

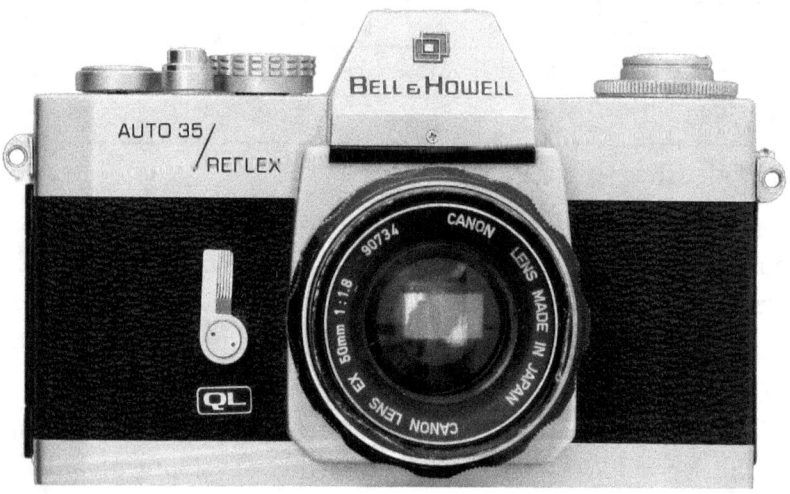

Near the end of the distribution agreement, collaboration between Canon and Bell & Howell produced an historically interesting camera, the FD35. Noting the camera's similarity to the Canon TX, some collectors have suggested that the FD35 is merely a rebadged TX. A closer look shows that the FD35 preceded the TX by nearly two years. Informed speculation suggests that Bell & Howell asked Canon to produce a modified TLb with a hot shoe and the company responded with the FD35. Apparently, that fulfilled Canon's commitment to Bell & Howell and Canon continued to produce the TX after the distribution agreement lapsed.[2]

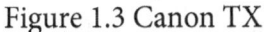

Figure 1.3 Canon TX

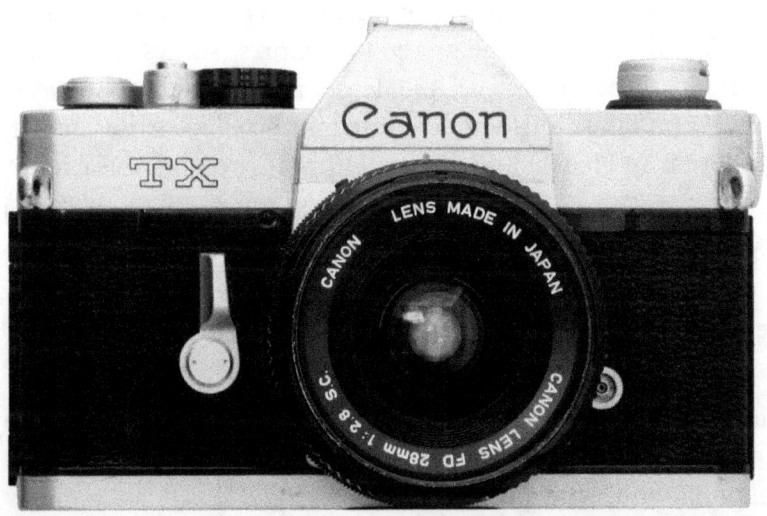

Revenue from camera sales funded technological development and Canon emerged from Leica's shadow during the 1960s. Canon rangefinder cameras and lenses were among the best available. Even Leica cameras were refitted to mount the spectacular Canon 50mm f0.95, the fastest production camera lens of its era.

While Canon owned large segments of the rangefinder camera market, new technologies and changing photographic tastes led the company to expand into single lens reflex cameras.

In 1954, Leica introduced its M3 rangefinder. New technologies produced bright viewfinder images and extraordinarily accurate focusing. Canon engineers recognized that matching the M3 would be a daunting task.

Simultaneously, macro and nature photography became increasingly popular and single lens reflex cameras are more suitable for both. SLRs focus and frame through the lens while rangefinder designs rely on separate

2 I am indebted to Gordon Yee for explaining this sequence. For the full argument, please see http://photo.net/canon-fd-camera-forum/00VMif.

viewing and focusing optics. Barely noticable in most activities, the offset between lenses and focusing optics is problematic when the camera is very close to the subject as in macro photography.

At the other extreme, nature photographers prefer long lenses to keep distance from dangerous animals and to compress scenes. Because SLRs focus and frame through the lens, long lenses are easy to use. Conversely, the optics in 35mm rangefinder cameras are optimized for lenses on the order of 35 to 85mm and lenses longer than 135mm are scarcely usable.

Canon and other manufacturers recognized these difficulties and developed some technically interesting solutions. For macro photography, Canon offered auto-ups to reduce minimum focusing distance and paramenders to reposition the camera body after focusing. For nature photographers, Canon offered mirror boxes to facilitate use of long lenses.[3]

Photographers did not warm to any of these accessories and many many people came to think of rangefinder cameras as "obsolete." The general public and many professionals saw single lens reflex cameras as the future of photography. Canon continued to produce rangefinders and lenses through the 1960s, but the company's development efforts increasingly concentrated on single lens reflex designs.

The Manual Focus SLR Era

Single lens reflex cameras soon dominated the market and Leica was one of very few companies that continued to produce high quality rangefinder cameras. Canon introduced its first SLR, the Canonflex, in 1959 along with a series of lenses using the new R mount. Through 1962, Canon produced four Canonflex models and 21 R-mount lenses. Not surprisingly, Canon emphasized long lenses and 14 of the 21 R mount lenses were 100mm or longer. The lineup even included a spectacular 2000mm

---

3 Auto-Ups combine close up filters with a magnifying lenses over the viewing lenses and reduce the focusing distance to as little 3.25 inches. Paramenders mount between the camera body and tripod or stand. After focusing on a close-up subject, flicking a lever moves the body to compensate for the offset between the viewing and taking lenses. Mirror boxes or "reflex mirror housings," mount between a rangefinder body and taking lens to permit viewing and focusing through the taking lens.

lens: nearly 24 inches long, 9.6 inches in diameter, and weighing over 23 pounds.[4]

The Canonflexes were welcome additions to Canon's line up, but simply could not compete with the legendary Nikon F series. Introduced in the same year, the Nikons featured interchangeable focusing screens, mirror lock up, 100% viewfinders, and an easy to use depth of field button. Ironically, the most novel Canonflex feature—a bottom mounted film advance lever—appealed to few photographers. Most prefer to keep one hand on the lens and the other near the shutter release button.

Nikon's dominance is evident from the respective cameras' histories. Nikon continued to produce the F until 1974 while the Canonflex lasted barely 5 months. The three subsequent Canonflex models had production lives almost as short and Canon found itself playing catch up through the early 1960s.[5]

In 1964, Canon introduced a modified lens mount, the FL, and the first of three cameras that helped to secure the company's future. Like the automatic R-mount lenses, FL-mount lenses have an aperture link between the lens and camera body.[6] This allows photographers to focus with apertures wide open and bright viewfinder images while lenses close to predetermined apertures when the shutter button is activated.

Simultaneously, the FX returned the film advance lever to photographers' preferred position atop the camera body, added an exposure meter (switchable between high and low ranges), offered shutter speeds between 1 and 1/1000 second and had a viewfinder with over 90% coverage.

In 1965, Canon introduced the Pellix featuring a fixed semitransparent mirror. The mirror directs about 1/3 of light entering the lens to the

---

4 All of the Canon "R" lenses from 300mm to 1000mm require the use of the Canon Bellows R for focusing. In addition, some require the use of the Canon Lens Supporter R and the proper Canon Intermediate Tube.

5   On a well-researched web page, Stephen Gandy notes that Canon produced roughly 17,000 Canonflexes and the remaining three models brought the total to around 125,000 units. In contrast, Nikon produced over 860,000 Fs. For more details, see http://www.cameraquest.com/canonflx.htm.

6 "Canonmatic" lenses have this feature, but standard R-mount lens apertures must be set manually.

viewfinder and the remainder to the film. This innovative design eliminates conventional moveable mirrors along with the noise they produce as well as blackouts when the shutter is actuated.

Figure 1.4 Canon FX

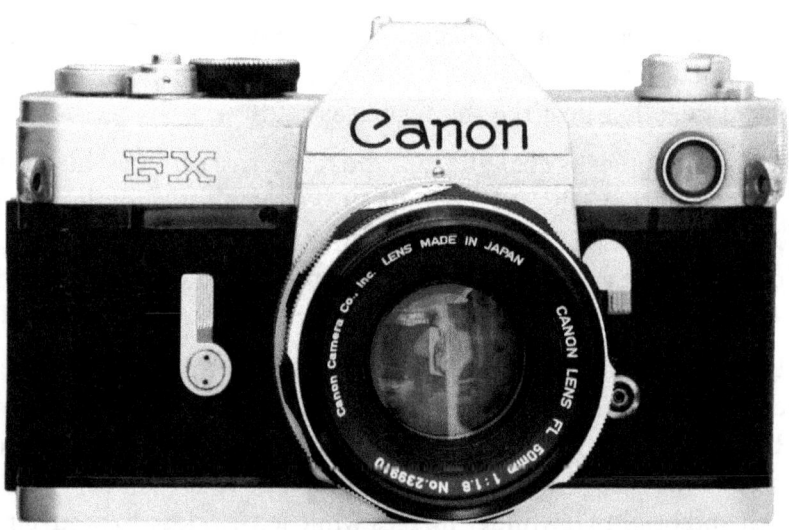

The Pellix also brought through the lens (TTL) metering to the Canon lineup.[7] In earlier designs, light meters measured light reflected by a portion of the scene approximating the view through a standard 50mm lens. Differences between light and dark areas typically average out with standard lenses and meter readings are good enough for most purposes. With longer lenses, however, disparities are problematic and photographers compensate as best they can. TTL metering eliminates the guesswork by reading light through the lens. This improves metering accuracy and users praised the reliability of Canon's new system.

Canon introduced the FTQL in 1966. The camera features a quick return mirror and TTL metering as well as a quick load system. The system

7 The Topcon RE Super had introduced full-aperture metering in 1963 and the Pentax Spotmatic offered stopped-down TTL metering a year before Canon introduced the Pellix.

has a stainless steel spring inside the film door to guide film into the take up sprocket. With it, photographers merely drop in the film canister, pull the leader across the film guides, close the door and advance the film.

The quick load system seems commonplace to modern photographers, but it was a remarkably important feature in the 1960s. Canon capitalized on its popularity by displaying a QL on selected cameras including the Pellix QL and the FT QL. The company also employed variants of the system on the FTb and FTbN as well as T series cameras other than the T60.

Figure 1.5 FT QL with Zoom Lens

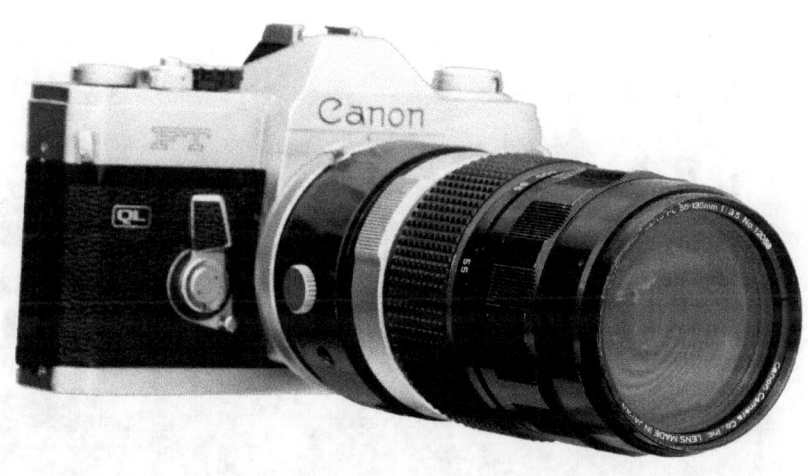

FL mount cameras were popular with consumers, but Canon still lacked a flagship professional camera. After 5 years of development, the company introduced a top of the line professional body, the F-1. Canon maintains that the time and effort invested in the F-1 was comparable to the effort required to develop ten or more conventional cameras. The F-1 is a mechanical camera that uses battery power only for metering. Solidly built to meet the needs of professional photographers, an F-1 is capable of 100,000 or more exposures in trying environments. Nearly 40 years after Canon distributed the first bodies, many continue to produce outstanding images in spite of scars from years of use. In addition to its solid build, the

F-1 is noteworthy for its line of accessories and the introduction of the FD lens mount.

Canon claims that more accessories were available for the F-1 than any other camera of the era. In addition to new FD mount lenses, the F-1 could use both FL- and some R-mount lenses. Other accessories included five interchangeable viewfinders, a motor drive with external battery pack, a data back and 250-shot film chamber, a magnifier and two angle finders, three flash couplers, and a comprehensive set of accessories for close-up photography.[8] Canon notes that "more than 180 accessories including lenses and filters were available for the F-1."

Figure 1.6 The Legendary F-1

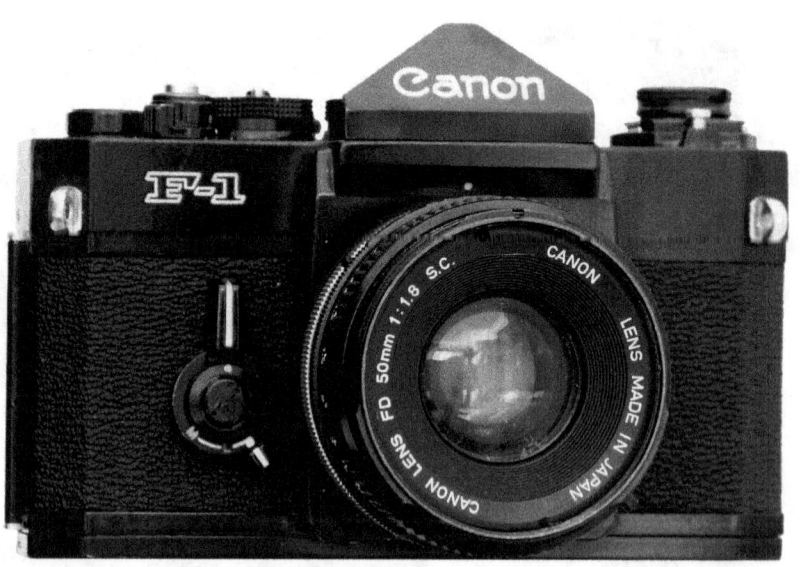

Canon developed the FD mount with an eye on the growing role of microelectronics. Whereas FL-mount lenses had a single pin to communicate operating aperture to the camera body, FD lenses have a second pin to

8 The list includes three bellows units, reversing rings and couplers, macro and micro photo hoods and couplers, copy stands, extension tubes, and 3 different focal length macro lenses. For details, please see Chapter 4.

register the maximum aperture. This addition permits full aperture metering and presages development of automatic metering.

In addition, Canon had high expectations for the new lenses. Development objectives included minimizing the number of elements, reducing flare, capturing uniformly high resolution, and reproducing natural colors.

As Canon anticipated, advances in microelectronics reshaped camera technology during the 1970s and 1980s. Canon kept pace with a series of products incorporating new technologies. Highlights include the following:

- In 1973, Canon introduced the EF with an electronic shutter, shutter speed-priority automatic exposure, and a silicon photocell meter.

- The AE-1 introduced in 1976 was the world's first camera with an embedded micro-computer. Canon promised that anyone could produce quality pictures and added automatic flash exposure with dedicated Speedlites as well as a power winder for continuous shooting at two frames per second.

- In 1982, Canon's AL-1 featured a focus assist system. LEDs visible in the viewfinder indicate whether or not the image is in focus and prompts the photographer to turn the focus ring in the correct direction.

The Autofocus Era

These developments paved the way for Canon's first autofocus SLR, the T80. Released in 1985, the T80 could use any FL- and FD- as well as some R-mount lenses. However, autofocus required specially built AC lenses of which Canon offered three: an AC50mm f1.8, AC35-70mm f3.5-4.5, and AC75-200mm f4.5. Based on a modified FD mount, the AC lenses have a rather unusual profile with an expanded housing on one side. The bulbous housing contains a somewhat bulky motor to move lens elements.

The T80 was a milestone for Canon, but the company was a step behind Minolta. Just two months before Canon released the T80, Minolta introduced the a-7000. In September, Minolta added the a-9000 while Nikon released the F-501 in April 1986. All three outperformed the T80 and Canon was nearly shut out of the market as demand for autofocus SLRs skyrocketed. By the end of April 1986, autofocus SLRs captured over 50% of the US SLR camera market.

Some authors believe that Canon went into a panic mode when the T80 stumbled. However that seems unlikely. Canon had probably begun development of advanced autofocus systems a couple years before introducing the T80. If so, the T80 was merely a stopgap body of technology demonstrator while Canon finished work on the EOS system.

Figure 1.6 Canon T80

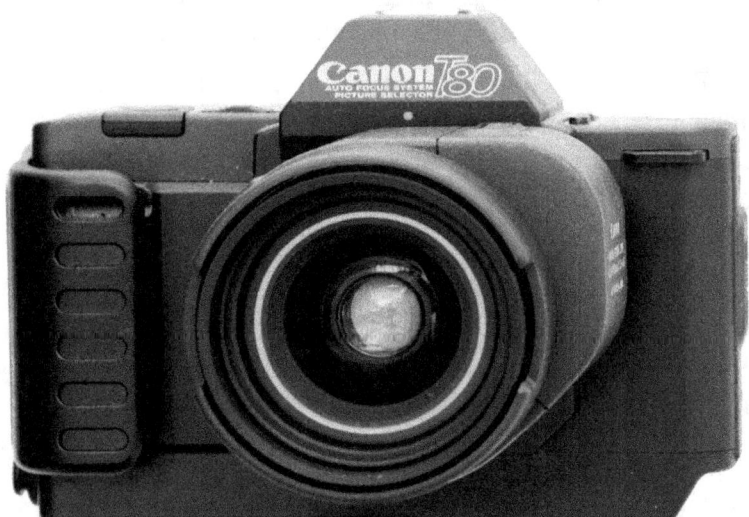

Simultaneously, Canon recognized that the FD lens mount was too small to accommodate the electronic contacts required for the next generation of cameras. Although the mount had been developed with an eye to future development, it was already three generations and nearly 20 years old when Canon introduced the EF lens mount.

The decision to abandon the FD mount in favor of the EF mount for the anticipated EOS (Electro-Optical System) was controversial. Many aficianados mourned the passing of the FD mount, largely because they had made substantial investments in lenses.[9] Nevertheless, Canon introduced its next generation EOS 650 in March, 1987. In May, Canon introduced an improved EOS 620 and further refinements followed in rapid succession; the EOS 750 QD in October 1988, the EOS 630 in April 1989, and the flagship EOS-1 in September 1989. All featured rapid autofocus and totally electrical communication between the bodies and a rapidly expanding list of EF lenses.

End of the Line

The introduction of the EOS line marked an important transition for Canon. Although the company concentrated on new autofocus cameras, it brought a handful of new manual focus SLRs to market. The remarkable T90 was introduced about a year before the EOS 650 (February 1986) and it had a number of attractive features. The T90 had three metering systems, eight auto exposure (AE) modes, two manual exposure modes and an integrated motor drive in a beautifully contoured body. As impressive as it is, the T90 was the culmination of earlier developments and its most attractive features easily moved into the EOS line.

The Cosina-made T60 was Canon's last manual focus SLR. It came to market in April 1990 more than three years after the EOS 650. Marketed to price conscious consumers, it was a last gasp manual focus camera.

Canon quickly dropped the T60 and ceased production of the T90 in late 1991. The New F-1 was the only Canon manual focus SLR produced thereafter. The company continued to support some manual focus SLRs and FD lenses until 2004. Bodies and lenses in the distribution channels continued to sell until stocks were exhausted. Nevertheless, the popularity of EOS cameras was the death knell for manual focus SLRs. Dedicated photographers continued to use the manual focus systems for a while, but many "traded up" when they could. Manual focus bodies and lenses migrated down to students and occasional users. Eventually, they moved into forgotten niches in closets, garages, and storage facilities.

---

9 As one critic notes, Canon treats its customers better than many other companies. Although the EF mount is nearly 35 years old, early EF lenses are still functional on advanced EOS film and digital bodies.

Dating Your Canon Manual Focus Gear

In 1960, Canon began using alphanumeric codes indicating when and where bodies, lenses, and major accessories were produced. You will probably need a strong light to see the black on black codes. They are located in film chambers on bodies, rear mounts of lenses, and inconspicuous spots on major accessories.

Figure 1.7 Canon T90 with 50f1.8

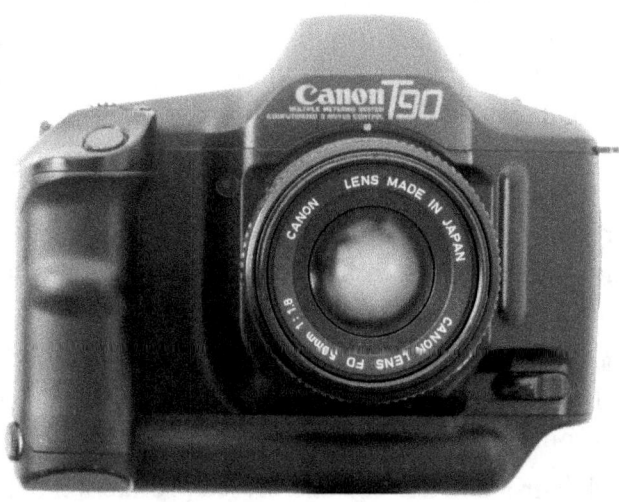

The six digit codes generally begin with a letter followed by four digits and a concluding letter. "N1148F" is typical. The first letter identifies the year of manufacture ("N" =1973), the first two digits indicate the month of production ("11"=November), the next two digits are an internal code of little interest to collectors, and the concluding letter denotes the factory ("F"= Fukushima).[10] The year code begins with A for 1960 and runs

10 Collectors have reported a few bodies without the internal code as well as some other variations. Canon evidently dropped leading zeros on the month codes from some early bodies as well as on lenses, and accessories. As a result, some codes have only one letter and three digits, but the pattern is otherwise intact. For additional details, see http://www.ehow.com/how_6661089_date-canon-a1-camera.html or http://www.bobatkins.com/photography/eosfaq/DATECODE.HTM..

sequentially through Z for 1985 and then restarts with A in 1986. Month codes run from 1 for January through 12 for December and factory codes include F for Fukushima and O or OI for Oita.

Conclusion

While technological development ended in the 1980s, there has been a resurgence of interest in Canon manual focus SLRs. Compared to today's plastic digital cameras with working lives of less than 2 years, it is a pleasure to hold a solid manual focus SLR that continues to produce impressive images nearly 50 years after it was produced.

Many FD and FL lenses are at work again thanks to relatively inexpensive adapters. Many are exceptionally sharp and produce images with distinctive color casts. In addition, manual focusing forces photographers to slow down and think about the images before pressing the shutter button.

Chapter 2: Canon Manual Focus SLR Bodies

Canon produced roughly 34 distinct manual focus SLRs between 1959 and the early 1990s.[1] Aside from unmarked variations, most bodies are clearly labeled and easily recognized. Counterfeiting has yet to become a significant problem,[2] but ill-informed sellers occasionally misrepresent their goods. As a collector, you need to look closely because some variations are more desirable and command significantly higher prices than others. For example, median prices for the three F-1s currently center around $160, $225, and just over $300. In addition, limited production and commemorative "editions" may also command significantly higher prices than standard models. For example, a limited edition "high speed" F-1 has recently been offered at more than $11,000.[3]

Finally, Canon sold several models in two color schemes. Chrome with black wraps for consumers and black painted models targeting professionals. Black models currently command a premium of about 50% and the most prized black bodies are the Canonflex RP, Canonflex RM, FX, FP, Pellix, and Pellix QL.[4]

Here are the principle variations for which you should watch:

- Collectors commonly recognize 3 versions of the F-1: the "original F-1" introduced in 1971, an upgraded version in 1976 and a substantially new camera in 1981. Collectors refer to the models as the F-1 or original F-1; the F-1 later model, second model, or F-1n; and the New F-1 or F1-N.[5]

---

1 As you will see below, the precise number depends on how collectors account for variations.

2 As noted earlier, a few unscrupulous sellers may be trying to convert standard chrome bodies into more desirable black bodies. In addition, some very obvious fakes have come on the market recently, but they are unlikely to mislead serious collectors.

3 The seller says that fewer than 100 were made and the number is cited on a handful of web sites. However, I have not otherwise confirmed his number.

4 All T-Series cameras are black owing to their polycarbonate housings and do not command a premium. Canon has not released either the number or distribution of black bodies. Estimates range from 1% to 5% and this enumeration is based on bodies in my collection as well as other reliable collector reports.

5 A few collectors also recognize early versions of the F-1 as a variant. The earliest bodies required modification to mount a motor drive.

- Canon introduced the FTb in 1971 and a newer model in 1973. Collectors refer to the second model as the New FTb or FTb-N. However, many sellers overlook the distinction.

- The EF was a state of the art electronic camera when it was introduced in 1973. Subsequently, Canon changed the focusing screen from plain matte to a split image rangefinder. The generally accepted transition point is at serial number 330,000, however collectors have identified bodies as low as 282,xxx with split image screens.[6]

- Canon produced specially badged commemorative editions of the F-1 for the 1976 Montreal Olympics, the 1980 Lake Placid Winter Olympics, and 1984 Los Angeles Olympics.[7] The company also produced commemorative 55mm and 58mm lens caps for the 1976 Montreal Olympics and 52mm lens caps for the Lake Placid games along with 55mm and 52mm lens caps commemorating the 1978 and 1982 soccer World Cups. In addition, in 1978 Canon produced a handful of military models designated "ODF-1" with an olive drab finish.

- Canon had a marketing agreement with Bell and Howell for 10 years (1962-1972). Some imported bodies are marked with both Canon and Bell and Howell while others have only the distributor's name. In addition, kits often combined Canon lenses with Bell and Howell badged bodies and subsequent users have regularly mixed the units. At the present time, Bell and Howell bodies command a modest premium and are the focus of increasing collector interest.[8]

---

6 In addition, Canon made occasional changes to the electronic circuitry. There may have been as many as six variations, but they are not evident on casual inspection and few collectors consider the differences to be significant. For example, see the discussion thread at http://photo.net/canon-fd-camera-forum/00XWWd.

7 Canon was the official camera sponsor for the Los Angeles Games and aimed to make the commemorative F-1 special. The standard version boasted gold paint for the camera designation and the Olympic Games emblem as well as the Canon name on the supplied AE Finder FN. In addition, serial numbers for the commemorative bodies began with LA.

8 As noted in Chapter 1, Canon had an earlier agreement with C.R. Skinner in San Francisco. In addition, the company may have had an earlier distribution with Scopus, Inc. See http://www.cameraquest.com for limited additional information.

Figure 2.1 lists Canon manual focus SLRs in chronological order. Asterisks designate models for which there are significant variations and the column labeled "Desirability" indicates the significance of each as a collectible. As you run your finger down the column, please remember the factors discussed in the Introduction. Collectors' personal interests and the condition of individual pieces are important factors and any body could reasonably be included in a collection of Canon manual focus SLRs.

More nearly universal criteria include historical significance, original quality, and rarity. On the basis of these factors, the table clusters desirability in four categories:

A = Highly desirable, a welcome addition to any camera collection

B = Desirable, a welcome addition to any Canon collection

C = Moderately desirable, a nice addition to larger Canon collections

D = Less desirable, appeals primarily to collectors who aim to complete a set.

Judgements in the table based on these criteria are mine alone, but they are generally consistent with those of other knowledgeable collectors. Historical significance weighs heavily in my view and I generally rate the first body with a particular feature or function higher than subsequent models. In addition, my view is that of a collector. Users value other factors and would probably produce very different ratings.

While the number of bodies is impressive, Canon produced most SLRs in "families" based on the same chassis. For example, the Canonflexes have the same body with some modifications and the entire FL family is based on the FX chassis. This manufacturing strategy helped Canon produce cameras at different price points while minimizing design, tooling and set-up costs.

The pages following the table summarize important collector information about each family of Canon manual focus SLRs.

Figure 2.1: Canon Manual Focus SLRs[9]

Model	Introduced	Discon-tinued	Lens Mount	Colors	Desir-ability
Canonflex	1959	1960	R	Chrome	A
Canonflex R 2000	1960	1962	R	Chrome	A
Canonflex RP	1961 (1960)[9]	1962	R	Chrome Black	B A
Canonflex RM	1962	1964	R	Chrome Black	C A
Canonex	1963	1964	Fixed	Chrome	B
FX	1964	1969	FL	Chrome Black	B A
FP	1964	1966	FL	Chrome Black	B A
Pellix	1965	1966	FL	Chrome Black	A A
FT QL	1966	1972	FL	Chrome Black	A A
Pellix QL	1966	1970	FL	Chrome Black	B A
TL QL	1967	1972	FL	Chrome	B
EX EE	1968 (1969)[9]	1973	Front Element	Chrome	B
F-1*	1971	1976	FD	Black	A
FTb *	1971	1973	FD	Chrome Black	A A

---

9 Canon's online museum does not include end-of-production dates and I've relied on Peter Dechert's dates. In addition, there are discrepancies in initial production dates for the Canonflex RP, EX EE, and TLb. For these models, I've used Dechert's dates with the museum dates in parentheses.

Model	Introduced	Discon-tinued	Lens Mount	Colors	Desir-ability
F-1 High Speed Motor Drive	1972	Special Order	FD	Black	B
EX Auto	1972	1976	Front Element	Chrome	B
EF *	1973	1977	FD	Black	A
FTb-N*	1973	1977	FD	Chrome Black	B A
TLb	1972 (1974)[9]	1977	FD	Chrome	C
TX	1975	1978	FD	Chrome	C
AE-1	1976	1984	FD	Chrome Black	A A
AT-1	1976	1982	FD	Chrome	B
F-1n*	1976	1981	FD	Black	B
A-1	1978	1987	FD	Black	A
AV-1	1979	1983	FD	Chrome Black	C B
AE-1 Program	1981	1987	FD	Chrome Black	B B
New F-1*	1981	1992	FD	Black	B
AL-1	1982	1985	FD	Chrome Black	B B
T50 (T-5)	1983	1987	FD	Black	B
New F-1 High Speed Motor Drive	1984	Special Order	FD	Black	B
T70	1984	1987	FD	Black	A
T80	1985	1986	FD (AC)	Black	B
T90	1986	1991	FD	Black	A
T60	1990	1990	FD	Black	D

The Canonflexes

Canonflex is the generic name for Canon's first family of manual focus SLRs. Starting with the original Canonflex in 1959, Canon produced four distinct models including the Canonflex, Canonflex R 2000, Canonflex RP, and Canonflex RM. All use the then-new R lens mount, have horizontal-travel focal plane shutters with cloth curtains, and viewfinders with approximately 0.9x magnification.

The cameras were well built and well finished, but circumstances mentioned in the Introduction doomed them. The second model, the Canonflex R 2000, had the shortest production run with fewer than 9,000 produced and is the most desirable for collectors. Around 17,000 of the original model were produced and it is also highly collectible. With around 31,000 produced, the Canonflex RP was the economy model and the least desirable collectible. The Canonflex RM is a substantially new camera with around 72,000 produced making it the most common body. However, it introduced new features including a built-in light meter that make it attractive to Canon collectors.

Figure 2.2: Canonflex Bodies

Body	Shutter Speeds	Battery	Mirror Lock Up	Self Timer	Exposure Modes
Canonflex	X, B_T and 1 to 1/1000	None	No	Yes	Manual
Canonflex R2000	T, B and 1 to 1/2000	None	No	Yes	Manual
Canonflex RP	X, B, and 1 to 1/000	None	No	Yes	Manual
Canonflex RM	X, B, and 1 to 1/1000	None	No	Yes	Manual

Canonflex The first "Flex" has an interchangeable pentaprism with a normal pentaprism and upright direct viewer with adjustable diopter correction. The external selenium exposure meter is switchable between high (EV 10-19) and low (EV 4-13) ranges. Film advances with a bottom trigger and there is no accessory shoe. Older flash units such as the Model V could be attached to a side-mounted bayonet. The body has a built-in self-timer and shutter button lock.

Canonflex R2000 is a deluxe version of the original Canonflex. It features a top shutter speed of 1/2000 and Canon combined the X Synch with 1/60 on the shutter speed dial to make room for the new top speed. It also has a fixed eye-level pentaprism, but is identical to the original Flex in other respects and can use the same external meter as the original. In addition, Canon offered a second external meter with a 1/2000 top speed.

Canonflex RP is an economy or "Populaire" version of the Flex and has a fixed, eye-level pentaprism viewfinder. It also has an eyepiece designed for easy use of correction lenses and uses the same external meter as its predecessors. It is the last Canon SLR with the bottom trigger and differs from the original Canonflex in modest particulars: no time exposure lock, "B-T" on the shutter speed dial became "B" and there is a flanged eyecup holder.

Canonflex RM uses a body shell similar to its predecessors, but differs in several respects. It has a fixed eye level pentaprism with a low profile and the top cover is elevated to accommodate a film advance lever. It is also the first Canon manual Focus SLR with an internal exposure meter.[10] The built-in meter uses a selenium photocell coupled to the speed dial with a range from EV 6 to 17 and accommodates films from ISO 10 to 800. It also has a built-in self-timer and shutter button lock.

FL Mount Bodies

With commercial failure of the Canonflexes, Canon recognized the need to restart their SLR line. They responded with a new lens mount—the FL mount, and a new group of bodies based on a common chassis. All feature horizontal travel focal plane shutters, fixed eye-level pentaprisms with 0.9x magnification, and all but the Pellix have cloth shutters. The Pellix and Pellix QL have metal shutter curtains.

---

10 The RM meter does not meter through the lens. The Pellix introduced three years later was the first Canon SLR with TTL metering.

The FX was released in 1964 while Canon rangefinder cameras were still in production. Peter Dechert finds it curious that the FX shares few parts with the Canon 7 or other rangefinder bodies. To me, however, it appears that Canon engineers deliberately chose to launch a new family of bodies. The FX chassis is the foundation of all FL mount cameras and the FT QL and TL survived into the FD era in four derivative models: the FTb, FTb-N TLb, and TX. Thus the extra costs incurred by Canon designers were amortized over three generations that remained in production until 1978.

Figure 2.3: FL Mount Bodies

Body	Shutter Speeds	Battery	Mirror Lock Up	Self Timer	Exposure Modes
FX	X, B and 1 to 1/1000	PX625	No	Yes	Manual
FP	X, B and 1 to 1/1000	None	No	Yes	Manual
Pellix	X, T and 1 to 1/1000	PX625	No	Yes	Manual
FT QL	X, T and 1 to 1/1000	PX625	No	Yes	Manual
Pellix QL	X, T and 1 to 1/1000	PX625	No	Yes	Manual
TL QL	X, B and 1 to 1/500	PX625	No	No	Manual

The **FX** has a CdS exposure meter on the photographers' left side of the body. It switches between low (EV1-10) and high (EV 9-18) ranges and accommodates films rated from ISO 10 to 800. The accessory shoe lacks electrical contacts and flash is supported by a PC socket on the camera front with an X-sync at 1/55. The viewfinder has a split-image rangefinder at center of a fresnel matte screen and mirror lockup provided.

The **FP** is a virtual clone of the FX with a slightly different film door lock and lacking an exposure meter. It could be fitted with an external meter matching the same specs as the FX's built-in meter.

Based on the FX chassis and mechanically identical to it aside from differences in the mirror, the **Pellix** introduced two important features. It is the first Canon SLR with TTL metering and the CdS cell reads a 12% area at the center of the viewfinder to support stopped-down metering with a range of EV 1 to 18. It accommodates films rated at ISO 10 to 800. Second, the Pellix introduced a stationary pellicle mirror splitting in-coming light. Roughly 1/3rd goes to the viewfinder while the remaining 2/3 exposes the film. The camera also uses metal shutter curtains and adds an eyepiece shutter.

Peter Dechert considers the **FT QL** to be "Canon's first major contribution to 35mm SLR design." His praise centers on the unique "Quick Load" feature which makes loading film much easier. In addition, the FT QL incorporates a CdS exposure meter reading off a 12% spot in the center of the viewfinder. The metering range is EV 3 to 18 and the system accommodates film rated from ISO 25 to 2000.

The **Pellix QL** is an upgraded Pellix with the QL feature as well as modifications to support use of a meter booster. There is also a lock to hold the metering cell in place while the photographer adjusts exposure and improved labeling on the eyepiece shutter. Like the original, the CdS cell meters on a 12% center spot, reads from EV 3 to 18, and supports films from ISO 25 to 2000.

The **TL QL** is a simplified and cheaper version of the FT QL with a top speed of 1/500. Like the FT QL, it offers TTL metering on a 12% spot at the center of the viewfinder and reads exposure values from EV 3.5 to 17. It also accommodates films rated at ISO 25 to 2000. Unfortunately, the entry in Canon's online museum has generated some confusion. The entry says "The camera was without a self-timer and QL feature . . . Although most TL cameras did not have QL, some cameras did as shown in the photo." The displayed image clearly displays the QL designation.[11] Peter Dechert maintains that the TL lacked only "the FT's 1/1000 shutter speed, mirror lock-up facility, battery check button, and shutter release lock. Other than these deletions, [he says] it was exactly the same." Collectors side with

11 Two threads on PhotoNet.com discuss this confusion in greater detail, see: http://photo.net/canon-fd-camera-forum/00XXTq and http://photo.net/canon-fd-camera-forum/00XWCA.

Dechert and none report finding a TL without the QL feature. TLs in my collection all have the quick load feature as do recent eBay listings.

Direct Descendents

Canon introduced the FD lens mount in 1971. With the new mount, the company introduced two now legendary cameras—the F-1 and FTb. The highly regarded EF followed just two years later while the FTb-N, TLb, and TX round out the series.

We will pick up the F-1 story in another section. For the time being, we can say that all except the F-1 and EF have mechanical, horizontally travelling focal plane shutters with cloth curtains as well as fixed, eye-level pentaprisms with 0.85X magnification, and built in CdS meters reading a 12% area in the center of the viewfinders. All support full-aperture metering with FD lenses and stopped down-metering with FL lenses. Aside from the EF and the final F-1 (the F-1N), all are fully mechanical cameras and batteries are needed only for the meters.

Figure 2.4 Direct Descendents

Body	Shutter Speeds	Battery	Mirror Lock Up	Self Timer	Exposure Modes
FTb	B and 1 to 1/1000	PX625	Yes	Yes	Manual
EF	X, B and 30 to 1/1000	Two PX625	Yes	Yes	Shutter-priority AE
FTb-N	X, B and 1 to 1/1000	PX625	Yes	Yes	Manual
TLb	X, B and 1 to 1/500	PX625	No	No	Manual
TX	X, B and 1 to 1/500	PX625	No	No	Manual

Designed for advanced amateurs, the **FTb** has rubberized silk shutter curtains rather than the more expensive titanium curtains found on the

F-1. It meters from EV 2.5 to 18 and accommodates films rated from ISO 25 to 2000. It is a substantial camera and many professionals used it as a back up for their F-1s.

Peter Dechert describes the **EF** as "a black beauty" and it is popular with both collectors and users. User interest arises from a quirk of fate. Like other popular cameras of the era including the TLb, FTb, F-1 and F-1n, the EF uses now banned 1.35 volt mercury batteries (PX 625 or equivalent). Users of the other cameras face difficult choices and often elect to use hand-held meters, modify the bodies, use relatively expensive substitutes, or leave the cameras on the shelf. Unlike its contemporaries, the EF has a built in voltage regulator and works fine with readily available 1.5 volt non-mercury batteries. The voltage regulator is not the sole reason for the EF's popularity. Slightly larger than the TLb and FTbs, the EF feels like an F-1 and is more user friendly than many other cameras.

The EF uses a hybrid shutter and long exposures (from 1 second to 30 seconds) are controlled electronically while faster speeds are mechanically controlled. The Copal Square shutter is a vertical-travel, metal-curtain, focal-plane shutter. The metering range is EV -2 to 18 and accommodates films rated from ISO 12 to 3200.

The **FTb-N** is an upgraded version of the FTb displaying the shutter speed in the viewfinder. It is the last Canon SLR with the QL designation and retained the original faceplate. Canon collectors distinguish it from the first model by designating it the "new" model or FTb-N. Most characteristics are identical to the original FTb, but recognizable differences include a black plastic tip on the modestly reshaped rewind lever, a smaller black and white delayed action lever, and a black plastic spring loaded cover on the PC flash outlet. The FTb-N meters from EV 2.5 to 18 and accommodates films rated from ISO 25 to 2000.[12]

The **TLb** is a cheaper version of the FTb with a top shutter speed of 1/500. Fitted with a cheaper accessory shoe, the TLb supports flash only through a PC socket on the front. Metering is modestly center weighted

---

12 The metering range can be extended with second version of meter booster described in Chapter 4.

and reads a range from EV 3.7 to 17. It accommodates films rated from ISO 25 to 2000.

The **TX** was originally developed for Bell & Howell and labeled the FD35. Canon continued to produce the camera under its own name after the distribution agreement expired. It is virtually identical to a TLb with an added hot shoe. Metering is centerweighted averaging with a range of EV 3.7 to 17 and accommodates films rated from ISO 25 to 2000.

A Series Bodies

Canon launched the A Series with the AE-1 in 1976. All A Series cameras use FD-mount lenses, horizontal travel focal plane cloth shutters, and fixed eye-level pentaprism viewfinders with magnification between 0.82 and 0.87. In addition, the A-series cameras feature electronically controlled shutters with center weighted TTL full aperture metering and flash sync at 1/60 second. They are the first Canon SLRs that must have a battery to operate. A-Series cameras reflect the growing importance of electronic technology and Canon maintains that the AE-1 was the first camera with a built in microprocessor.

The AE-1 and A-1 are historically significant, landmark cameras and should be present in any collection. The AL-1 comes close to landmark status and deserves a place in larger Canon collections. Fortunately the three are relatively easy to find in today's marketplace at reasonable prices. The series remained in production until 1987 when the last AE-1 Program rolled off the assembly lines.

The **AE-1** is a landmark camera in several respects. Designed as an amateur camera, the AE-1 is the first fully electronically controlled SLR and it pioneered highly automated manufacturing as well as extensive use of plastic body parts. It is also the first consumer camera with an automatic exposure mode and automatic exposure compensation. Its metering range is EV 1 to 18 and with an exposure compensation range of +1.5 EV. It accommodates films rated from ISO 25 to 3200.

The **AT-1** is an economy model of the AE-1 produced solely for export. It uses the same body, but lacked auto exposure and reverted to center weighted TTL metering using a CdS photocell. The metering range is EV 3 to 17 and the camera accommodates films rated from ISO 25 to 3200.

Figure 2.5: A-Series Cameras

Body	Shutter Speeds	Battery	Mirror Lock Up	Self Timer	Exposure Modes
AE-1	X, B and 2 to 1/1000	PX28	No	Yes	Manual and shutter speed-priority AE
AT-1	X, B and 2 to 1/1000	PX28	No	Yes	Manual
A-1	X, B and 30 to 1/1000	PX28	No	Yes	Manual plus five AE modes
AV-1	X, B and 2 to 1/1000	PX28	No	Yes	Aperture priority
AE-1 P	B and 2 to 1/1000	PX28	No	Yes	Manual plus four AE modes
AL-1	X, B and 2 to 1/1000	Two AAA	No	Yes	Manual plus aperture priority AE

The **AV-1** is a simplified camera for entry-level users. It features shutter priority AE and users can select only X, B and auto shutter speeds. The metering range is EV 1 to 18 and the camera accommodates films rated from ISO 25 to 1600. X & B are manually selectible, but other speeds are set by the camera

The **AE-1 Program** expands the AE-1's capabilities and offers four auto exposure modes: shutter speed-priority AE, program AE, preset aperture-priority AE, and Speedlite AE. In addition, the AE-1P sports a palm grip like the top of the line A-1. It also has three external electrical contacts (1 more than the original AE-1) to support use of the new Motor Drive MA. The camera can also use the original Winder A as well as the newer A2. The camera sold with a split prism rangefinder with double diffraction prism at the center of laser matte screen. Eight user changeable focusing screens are interchangeable through the mirror box. The metering range is EV 1 to 18 and accommodates films rated from ISO 12 to 3200.

The **A-1** sits atop the A-Series and Peter Dechert describes it as "robust [and] ruggedly handsome." He maintains that the A-T dial for switching between aperture and shutter priority modes had a lasting impact on modern camera design. The A-1 features manual plus five AE modes: shutter speed-priority AE, aperture-priority AE, program AE, preset aperture-priority AE, and Speedlite AE (with dedicated Speedlite). In addition, there are six technician-interchangeable focusing screens and comprehensive digital LED viewfinder read-outs displaying shutter speeds, apertures, manual metering indications, and warning signals. The built-in TTL meter reads from EV-2 to 18, has an exposure compensation range of 2 EV and accommodates films rated from ISO 6 to 12,800 in 1/3 steps.

The **AL-1** is the last of the A series cameras and introduced a unique focus alert system that paved the way for Canon's autofocus cameras. Designed for users with difficulty focusing through the viewfinder, the system searches for the subject's peak image contrast from three linear CCD arrays. The bottom of the viewfinder has arrows indicating the direction to turn the focusing ring to achieve focus. When focus is achieved, the in-focus mark between the two arrows lights. Viewfinder information includes focusing frame, in-focus indicator (red/green LED), exposure meter needle, shutter speed scale, overexposure and underexposure warnings, battery check index, and camera shake warning. The metering range is EV 1 to 18 although the focus alert functions only above EV3.5. The camera accommodates films rated from ISO 25 to 1600. Speeds below 1/15 are only electronically selected by the camera.

T Series Bodies

Canon's T series consists of five cameras noted for their sculpted polycarbonate bodies, extensive automation, and integration of electronic controls. All use FD lenses and all have fixed eye-level pentaprisms with magnification on the order of 0.85X, silicon photocell TTL metering, vertical travel focal plane electronic shutters and all but the T60 have integrated winders. The family includes the T50 which received the Good Design Award from the Ministry of International Trade and Industry in 1983, the T80–Canon's first autofocus SLR, and the T90–Canon's most sophisticated manual focus SLR as well as the popular T70 and "last gasp" T60 manufactured by Cosina.[13]

Figure 2.6: T-Series Bodies

Body	Shutter Speeds	Battery	Mirror Lock Up	Self Timer	Exposure Modes
T50 (T-5)	2 to 1/1000	Two AA	No	Yes	Programmed AE and programmed flash AE
T60	B plus 8 to 1/1000	Two LR44	No	Yes	Manual or aperture-priority AE mode.
T70	B plus 2 to 1/1000	Two AA	No	Yes	Manual plus four AE modes
T80	B, 1/60 and 2 to 1/1000	Four AA	No	Yes	Manual, stopped down AE and 5 AE modes
T90	B, 1/60 and 30 to 1/4000	Four AA	No	Yes	Manual plus 7 AE modes

The **T50 (T-5)**[14] is a greatly simplified camera with little user control. Programmed auto exposure is the default mode. Manual exposure is limited to 1/60 of a second with the user selecting the aperture. Like the AV-1, there is no manual option and only aperture priority exposure is available. It is noteworthy as Canon's first SLR with integral winder. The metering range is EV 1 to 18 and supports films rated from ISO 25 to 1600. Coincidentally, production ended in 1987, but Canon may have made a batch in 1990 while finalizing the T60 design.

13 Three earlier cameras have names beginning with the letter "T:" the TX, TL and TLb. All three predate the T Series and are discussed above as Direct Descendents of the FL Bodies.

14 The T-5 is a private label version of the T50 sold through U.S. Military Post Exchanges.

The **T60** is not important historically and has little in common with the other T-Series cameras. It was introduced three years after the EOS system as the final camera in the T-Series. Light and compact, the T60 is easy to carry and use, but has a less than stellar reputation. Reliability problems are attributed to uneven quality control at Cosina which manufactured the camera on behalf of Canon. Peter Dechert calls it "an afterthought" and notes that it was a simple, basic camera for students and people who could not afford an autofocus SLR. It is the only T Series camera without an integral winder. The metering range is EV 2 to 18 and the camera accommodates films rated from ISO 25 to 1600.[15]

The **T70** is an extraordinarily capable camera and Peter Dechert describes it as a T version of the A-1. It is the first Canon camera with an external LCD screen displaying all functions and it pioneered the use of buttons to control essential functions. Many professional photographers carried the T70 as a backup body. It offers manual plus four auto exposure modes: multi-program AE, shutter speed-priority AE, program flash AE, and TTL preset aperture A. Its metering range is EV 1 to 19 and can accommodate films rated from ISO 12 to 1600.

The **T80** is Canon's first commercial autofocus SLR. Using a linear CCD array for TTL image contrast detection derived from the AL-1 and three specially designed AC lenses, the T80 was a simple camera to operate. Exposure modes are selected from pictographs displayed on an external LCD screen and the camera offers manual and stopped down metering plus 5 programmed AE modes: standard, deep depth of field, shallow depth of field, stop action, and flowing. Its metering range is EV 1 to 19 with an exposure compensation range of 1.5 EV and the camera can accommodate films rated from ISO 12 to 1600.

The **T90** is Canon's most sophisticated manual focus SLR. Designed to automate the picture-taking process, the T90 targets relatively accomplished photographers and may overwhelm less capable users. Options include eight interchangeable focusing screens, three metering modes (centerweighted averaging, partial metering at center, spot metering at center), as well as seven auto exposure modes: standard program AE, variable shift

---

15 The Canon museum erroneously lists EV1 to 18.

program AE (with 7 program settings), shutter priority AE, aperture priority AE, stopped down AE, flash AE, stopped down metering, and manual. It is also noteworthy as Canon's first SLR with TTL flash metering when used with the dedicated Speedlite 300TL. Its metering range is EV 1 to 20 with an exposure compensation range of ±2 EV (in 1/3-stop increments) and can accommodate films rated from ISO 6 to 6400.

The F-1s

The F-1s are professional grade cameras suitable for the most demanding photographic tasks. The bodies are the centerpieces of comprehensive photographic systems with substantial numbers of accessories. Tested to 100,000 exposures, the F-1s can be used in extreme climates with temperatures from -30 degrees to +60 degrees Celsius.

Like other models, the F-1s are clearly marked and counterfeiting has yet to become a significant problem. However, a pair of marketing decisions complicate identification of specific models. In 1971, Canon promised to support the F-1 for a decade. Technology evolved faster than anticipated and in 1976 Canon introduced a modestly improved model. To maintain the initial promise, the company designated the improved model F-1 and did not add identifying marks to the updated body. Finally in 1981, Canon introduced a substantially new top-of-the-line camera with a hybrid electromagnetic and mechanical shutter, additional focusing screens and other enhancements. The changes are so substantial that most accessories from the earlier generations are not compatible with the new model and it would have made sense to rename the camera. Some collectors have speculated that F-2 would have been a better name. Canon, however, chose to retain the F-1 name, perhaps to avoid appearing to follow Nikon which already had an F-2.

Whatever the reasoning, the fact that three models carry the F-1 name is a source of some confusion. Collectors now refer to the three cameras as the F-1 or "original F-1," the F-1n or "later model," and the New F-1 or F-1N.[16] The variations are relatively easy to recognize once you know what

16 There is one other complication. Canon introduced the original F-1 before specifications for the Motor Drive Unit were firmly established. As a result, early production

to look for. Figure 2.7 summarizes the distinctive visual characteristics of each.

Figure 2.7 Distinguishing between the F-1s

	F-1	F-1n	F1-N
Top deck	Level	Level	Stepped*
Paint	Shiny	Shiny	Matte
Hot Shoe+	No	No	Yes
Serial Numbers	100001 to 317000	500001 to 675000	100001 to 312000
Top ASA	2000**	3200	6400
Film Reminder	No	Yes	Yes
Cocking Lever	Metal	Plastic Tip	Metal

* The two halves of the top plate on the F-1 and F-1n are level with one another. On the F-1N, the top plate on the photographers right steps up to accommodate the shutter release and film speed dial.
+ The first two F-1s use accessory couplers for flash while all but the two waist-level finders for the F-1n have hot shoes. See Chapter 4 for details.
**1600 is the highest shown on the dial.

The F-1 and F-1n are essentially mechanical cameras and use batteries only for the meters. The F-1N is an electronic camera using then state-of-the-art electromagnetic controls. Its hybrid shutter is electronically controlled at speeds below 1/90 and the camera incorporates two integrated circuits—an analog chip for metering and a digital chip controlling the shutter, self timer and meter read out.

In spite of the pronounced differences, the three F-1s have several features in common. All have interchangeable pentaprisms, horizontal travel focal plane shutters with metal curtains, and user interchangeable focusing screens. And all rely on accessories to achieve their full potentials.[17]

---

units with serial numbers from 100,000 to 199,000 will not accept the drive. For a while Canon modified the affected bodies for free and there is no information regarding the number of unmodified units remaining in circulation. The early variant should be highly collectible but few collectors recognize it.

17 Most accessories for the F-1 and F-1n are interchangeable. Accessories for the New F-1 are designated "FN" as in AE Finder FN and AF Motor Drive FN.

Figure 2.8: F-1 Bodies

Body	Shutter Speeds	Battery	Mirror Lock Up	Self Timer	Exposure Modes
F-1	X, B and 1 to 1/2000	PX625	Yes	Yes	Manual*
F-1n	X, B and 1 to 1/2000	PX625	Yes	Yes	Manual*
New F-1	X, B and 8 to 1/2000	PX26	No	Yes	Manual, Shutter Priority AE, and Aperture Priority AE
*Plus Shutter Priority AE with Servo EE finder.					

The original **F-1** is a top-of-the-line mechanical camera intended for professional use. It has four interchangeable focusing screens and is compatible with additional screens released with the F-1n. With a standard finder, it offers only manual exposure control while accessories add shutter priority auto exposure. Its metering range is EV 2.5 to 18 and it will accommodate films rated from ISO 25 to 2000.

The **F-1n** incorporates several modest functional improvements. The number of interchangeable focusing screens increased to nine, the film advance lever offset increased from 15 to 30 degrees and the winding stroke decreased from 180 to 139 degrees, the maximum ASA increased to 3200, the size of the shutter release cap increased and spring loading was added to the battery check switch. In addition, the mirror was modified to transmit more blue light, and screw in capability added to the PC socket. Aside from these changes, the F-1n remains a manual camera with a metering range from EV 2.5 to 18 and it accommodates films rated from ISO 25 to 3200.

The **New F-1** is a substantially new camera and it has more in common with A Series cameras than the first two F-1s. Its hybrid shutter has mechanical shutter speeds at B and X and from 1/125 to 1/2000 with electronically controlled slow speeds. "A" on the shutter speed dial invokes System Auto Exposure with aperture priority while shutter-speed priority requires either the Winder FN or Motor Drive FN. Three metering patterns (3% center spot metering, 12% partial center metering and centerweighted averaging) are available depending on the focusing screen in use and thirty-two optional interchangeable focusing screens are available. The metering range is EV 1 to 18 with exposure compensation from -2 to +2 EV and the camera accommodates films rated from ISO 6 to 6400.

The Others

In addition to the camera families described above, Canon marketed three manual focus SLRs with little evident relationship to the others. The group includes the very rare Canonex as well as the EX-EE and EX Auto.

Figure 2.8: Other MF SLR Bodies

Body	Shutter Speeds	Battery	Mirror Lockup	Self Timer	Exposure Modes
Canonex	B, 1/15 to 1/500	None	No	No	Manual and shutter speed-priority AE
EX EE	B plus 1/8 to 1/500	PX 625	No	Yes	Shutter speed-priority AE
EX Auto	B plus 1/8 to 1/500	PX 625	No	Yes	Shutter speed-priority AE

Canon produced fewer than 20,000 **Canonex** cameras and most were distributed in Europe. They are rare in the United States and highly collectible as a result of their unique features and rarity. Produced for just a year, the Canonex was Canon's first and last Lens-Shutter SLR camera. It features shutter speed-priority AE with a built-in selenium exposure meter, a Copal X shutter and a fixed 48mm f2.8 lens. Its metering range is EV 7 to 17 and accommodates film rated from ISO 10 to 400.

The **EX EE** was Canon's first SLR combining fully automatic exposure with interchangeable lenses. Designed for the amateur market, it is a peculiar camera in several respects. Equipped with the Quick Load system and a cloth focal plane shutter with a top speed of 1/500 second, the EX EE uses a unique lens system. A lens barrel is permanently fixed to the body and focal lengths are changed by screwing an interchangeable front element into the barrel. The front elements are clearly marked "Canon Lens EX" and Canon offered four: 50f1.8, the normal lens, 35f3.5, 95f3.5, and a 125f3.5.[18] The lenses have no aperture ring and apertures are set with a concentric ring around the film rewind knob. The metering range is EV 4.75 - 17 and the camera supports films rated from ISO 25 to 800.

More common cameras with interchangeable front lens elements typically have leaf shutters. Bob Shell speculates that Canon originally intended to use a leaf shutter with the EX EE, but substituted a focal plane shutter when they could not get it to function reliably.

Regardless of its design history, the EX-EE was popular enough to be marketed in a Bell & Howell version as the Auto35/Reflex. Experts agree that the EX EE was a capable camera and believe that there are relatively few in the collectible market because their owners "used them to death."

The **EX Auto** is an upgraded version of the EX EE launched four years earlier. It uses the same interchangeable front elements, but adds support for Canon's CAT electronic flash system. Updates include a hot shoe instead of the original's accessory shoe and a folding black lever for the CAT system on the fixed lens barrel. In addition, the flash socket was moved from the left end of the body to the side of the mirror box.

Conclusion

Between 1959 and 1994, Canon introduced 34 manual focus SLRs. The strategy of producing camera families contributed to the number, but it is still an enviable total.

Reliable autofocus cameras put an end to the manual focus era, but the transition was not swift. Canon officially discontinued the F-1N in 1994,

---

18 Front elements for the EX EE and EX Auto are marked with white lettering which makes them easy to distinguish from two EX lenses Canon produced for Exakta. Both the 135mm f3.5 and 100mm f3.5 Exakta lenses have red lettering.

but had already introduced more than 15 EOS models along with a substantial number of less sophisticated AF cameras.[19]

As autofocus cameras became the norm, manual focus gear migrated to students and others who did not need the most modern equipment. Eventually, even the best manual focus gear moved to boxes, closets and other storage areas.

Over the last decade or so, collectors and users have scoured the forgotten places. Many Canon manual focus SLRs have moved to more fitting homes–collectors cabinets and the working kits of photographers who consider film an "exotic" medium.

The pace of migration is a tribute to the quality of Canon's manual focus SLRs, but there is more to tell. Canon's manual focus lenses are at least as attractive as the bodies and the next chapter picks up their stories.

---

19 Canon has never released details, but it appears that the last F-1N was actually produced in 1992. Factory support ended in 2004.

Chapter 3: Canon Manual Focus Lenses

Collecting Canon manual focus lenses is at least as engaging as collecting bodies. Like the bodies, most lenses are well marked and counterfeiting has yet to become a major problem. Nevertheless, collecting lenses requires even greater attention to detail. There are more variations to choose from, some defects are harder to spot, and rare or exotic items are more difficult to find. Prices are higher than expected because users compete with collectors and some lenses typically sell for more than all but the most desirable bodies.

A quick glance at the ring around the front element of a Canon lens tells you much about it. For example, the lens pictured in Figure 3.1 declares itself to be a FD mount lens with a 50mm focal length, and maximum aperture of f1.8. "S.C." denotes Canon's "Spectra Coating." Other lenses may be designated R or FL and some use Roman Numerals to show that they are the second or even third version of a lens with similar optical specifications.

Figure 3.1 Representative Canon Lens

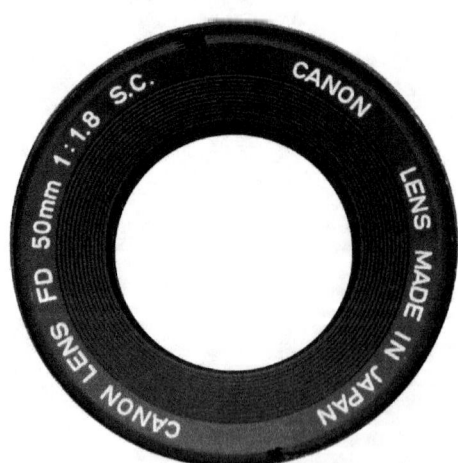

Lens Designations

Some Canon lenses have additional designations to show that they have special glass or coatings and that Canon used special care in manufacturing them.

Figure 3.2 Supplementary Lens Designations

Designation	Notes
S.C.	Denotes lenses with Canon's "Spectra Coating" designed to reduce flare.* The first lens designated "S.C." was the FD 28f3.5 S.C. introduced in March, 1973.+
S.S.C.	Marks lenses with Canon's "Super Spectra Coating." The first lens designated S.S.C. was the FD 7.5f5.6 S.S.C. introduced in February 1973. Coincidentally, virtually all of Canon's second generation FD lenses are multicoated (only the new FD 50 f1.8 was S.C. treated) and Canon discontinued use of the designation when it introduced the second generation of FD lenses in 1976.
AL	Denotes lenses incorporating an aspherical lens element, typically in a floating element design. The first AL lens marketed was the FD 55f1.2 in 1971.
Fluorite	Marks lenses with one or more fluorite elements to minimize dispersion. The designation was introduced in 1974 with the FL-F 300f2.8 S.S.C. Fluorite. Canon also produced FL-F300 f5.6 and FL-F 500f5.6 lenses.
L	Stands for "Luxury." By the mid 1970s, Canon realized that multiple lens markings were becoming confusing and settled on the L to mark premium lenses. The 300f4L introduced in 1978 was the first to carry the mark.

*Some Canon literature suggests that S.C. denotes a single layer coating. For example, the EF users guide says "Most lenses are now multi-layer coated with Canon's exclusive process, called Super Spectra Coating. S.S.C. indicates multi-layer coating, whereas S.C. (Spectra Coating) indicates single-layer coating." However, Canon literature is not entirely consistent and some collectors believe that S.C. is also a multi-layer process.

+Canon's museum dates are sometimes suspect. One collector has a copy of this lens with a production code date of November 1971.

Canon produced so many lenses and variations that not even Canon's online museum lists them all. Simply listing them would take far too many pages, but I'll refer to many while detailing the principal manual focus lens families, explaining some technical differences and compatibility issues, and identifying features that affect collectability.

Canon Manual Focus Lens Families

Canon produced four families of manual focus lenses plus two camera-specific sets. Canon introduced R mount lenses with the Canonflex in 1959 and the family includes both standard R and Super Canonmatic lenses. In 1964, Canon introduced a new series of lenses with FL mounts and seven years later brought out FD lenses. New FD mount lenses (abbreviated FDn) joined the line up in 1976 and remained in production until Canon discontinued manual focus SLRs.

The two camera-specific sets are designated EX and AC. Canon produced six EX lenses for the EX EE and EX Auto. The lenses remained in production until the EX Auto was discontinued in 1976.[1] Canon also produced three auto focus lenses for the T80. They are based on the FD mount and auto focus only when mounted on a T80 body. As we noted in the preceding chapter, the auto focus system was less capable than competitors from Minolta and Nikon, and Canon discontinued the family in 1986.

Figure 3.3 Canon Manual Focus Lens Families

Mount	Introduced	Details
R	1959	Introduced with the Canonflex, Canon produced 16 lenses from 35 to 200mm plus a 55-135mm zoom. Designed for Canonflex bodies, the R-mount lenses come in two flavors. Super Canonmatic lenses automatically cock the aperture when film is advanced while R lenses require manual cocking. Both offer limited compatibility with later models.

---

1 Coincidentally, in 1955 Canon produced a few 100mm and 135mm lenses in the Exacta mount. They are not compatible with the EX EE or EX Auto and are easily distinguished. The Exacta lenses are marked "EX" in red and have bayonet mounts whereas those of the EX EE and EX Auto are marked in white and have a screw mount.

Mount	Introduced	Details
FL	1964	Introduced with the FX, Canon produced 30 FL lenses from 19 to 1200mm plus three zooms.* Designed for the FL-mount bodies, FL lenses have limited compatibility with subsequent FD-mount bodies.
EX	1968	Introduced with the EX EE, EX lenses are interchangeable front elements that screw onto a barrel permanently fixed to the body. The family consists of six lenses from 35 to 125mm that are compatible only with the EX EE and EX Auto.
FD	1971	Introduced with the F-1, Canon produced 61 FD lenses from 7.5 to 800mm plus 7 zooms. Their most distinctive feature is a chrome locking ring that secures the lens to the camera. They are commonly referred to as "Chrome Nose" lenses and some authors designate them FD(A) lenses. They are compatible with all Canon manual focus bodies produced afterward except the EX EE and EX Auto. They have limited backward compatibility with FL mount and R mount bodies
FDn	1976	Introduced with the AE-1, Canon produced at least 42 FDn lenses from 7.5 to 800mm plus 23 zooms. They lack the distinctive chrome ring of the earlier FD lenses and the entire lens turns to secure it to a camera. Some collectors call them "Bayonet Mount" or FD(B) lenses and they are generally lighter than chrome nose lenses owing to the increased use of composites. They are compatible with all FD mount cameras and have limited compatibility with earlier bodies except the EX EE and EX Auto.

Mount	Introduced	Details
AC	1985	Introduced with the T80, Canon offered three auto focus lenses (50f1.8, 35-70f3.5-4.5 and 75-200f4.5).
*Longer FL lenses including a 5200mm f14 mirror lens were available by special order.		

Technical Differences and Compatibility

Aside from the EX lenses, all of Canon's manual focus SLR lenses have the same external mount dimensions. In addition, all are designed to eliminate wear on critical bearing surfaces. When mounted and dismounted, the points that determine distance to the film plane do not turn against one another and the critical distance remains constant no matter how often the lens is used.

While external dimensions and bayonet structures are the same, pins and levers that communicate with bodies are distinct. To illustrate the differences, we'll begin with the FD mount and work backwards. Figure 3.4 displays the back of an FD lens with five components labeled.

The reserved pin at 11 O'clock is a bit of an enigma. Canon has never disclosed its purpose and most collectors believe it was added to support functions that were never deployed as Canon migrated to the EF mount.

Figure 3.4 FD Lens Mount

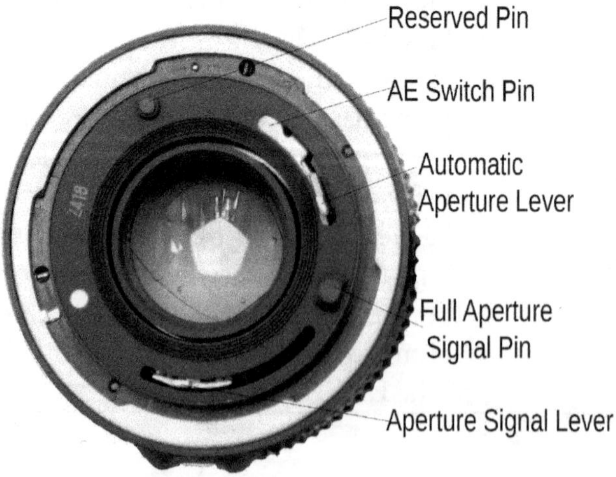

Reserved Pin

AE Switch Pin

Automatic Aperture Lever

Full Aperture Signal Pin

Aperture Signal Lever

The AE Switch Pin extends from the back of the lens when the aperture ring is set to A. This is a safeguard to prevent users from mounting the lens on bodies that do not support AE photography.

The Automatic Aperture Lever couple with the camera body to stop the lens down to a perset aperture just before the shutter releases.

The Full Aperture Signal Pin and Aperture Signal Lever transmit information to a camera's exposure meter. The first reports the lens' maximum aperture while the second indicates the len's preset aperture.

The FL mount is much simpler and features a single pin that mates with a lever in the camera's throat. Apertures are manually selected on the lens body and the pin closes it to the preselected value when the shutter is activated. There is no provision for communicating the selected aperture to the camera and TTL metering is accurate only with lenses manually stopped-down. Canon trailed both Nikon and Topcon in this regard and Peter Dechert argues that this shortcoming was responsible for Canon's economic woes for the next six years until it released the FD mount.

Canonflex lenses have two protruding pins at the rear. The first cocks the aperture spring mechanism when film is advanced while the second releases the aperture to the selected taking aperture when the shutter is activated.

In addition to its principal lens families, Canon introduced three auto focus lenses with the T80. Focus motors are mounted in an extended housing on the side of the lens. Viewed from the front, the lenses have a squashed tear drop profile.

Figure 3.5 50mm FD and AC Lenses

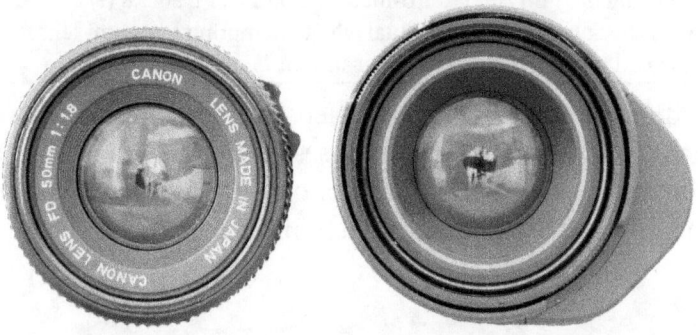

Because the lenses have common external mount dimensions, most Canon manual focus SLR lenses can be mounted on bodies other than those for which they were designed. However, differences in pin and lever layouts make some combinations impractical. Figure 3.6 provides a top level overview. Be sure to look carefully at your camera owners' guide as well as the notes in the table before mounting lenses on bodies other than those for which they were designed. Remember, some combinations may damage the camera, lens, or both.

Figure 3.6 Body and Lens Compatibilities

		Bodies				
		Canonflex	FL-Mount	EX-EE EX Auto	FD-Mount	T80
Lenses	R	Yes	Yes	No	Manual cocking required	
	FL	Yes	Yes	No	Stopped down metering only	
	EX	No	No	Yes	No	
	FD FDn	Not Recom- mended	Yes	No	Yes	
	AC		Yes	No	Not recom- mended	Yes

Some lenses extend into camera bodies and should be used only on bodies with mirror lock up. The FLP 38f2.8 pancake lens should be used only on Pellix bodies. In addition, Canon users' manuals regularly caution against use of selected lenses and note that some lenses require manual metering. For example, the FL 19f3.5 and FL 58 f1.2 cannot be mounted on the T90 while hand-held metering is required when using the FL 17f3.5 Retro-focus, FL 35f2.5, FL 50f1.8 (I) and FL 58f1.2 (II). Always check your camera manual when attempting to mount lenses other than the designated types and proceed with caution.

In addition to manual focus SLR lenses, Canon produced several related items of interest. Close-up lenses (AKA, "macro filters") and extension tubes are described in the chapter on Canon Accessories and the next few paragraphs describe teleconverters and macro lenses.

Teleconverters or tele-extenders are secondary lenses mounted between the camera and a photographic lens. Canon made three FD-mount tele-converters: the 1.4x-A, the 2x-A and the 2x-B.

The 1.4 increases the effective focal length of a lens by a factor of 1.4 and reduces light reaching the film by one f-stop. Both 2x models double the effective focal length and reduce light reaching the film by two f-stops. Minimum focusing distances remain unchanged and they support full-aperture metering as well as automatic diaphragm coupling.

Canon maintains that none of the teleconverters reduce the optical performance of its primary lenses. The company recommends using the 1.4x-A and 2x-A with fixed focal length lenses of 300mm or longer except the 300 f2.8L. They also recommend the A series teleconverters with the 200f4 macro as well as any zoom that reaches to 300mm or longer. For the 300f2.8L, Canon recommends using the 2x-B which is also recommended for prime and zoom lenses shorter than 300mm.

Canon also produced three lenses without internal focusing mechanisms for use with bellows. The Macrophoto 20mm f3.5 and Macrophoto 35mm f2.8 are capable of magnifying images 4 to 10 and 2 to 6 times life size respectively. With accessory duplicators 8 and 16, these lenses can be used to copy 8mm and 16mm images to standard 35 film. The earlier FL M 100mm F4 is also intended for use with bellows while the E50mm f3.5 is an S-mount lens for enlargers.

Figure 3.7 Canon Lenses for Bellows and Enlargers

Lens	Intro-duced	Construction (groups, elements)	Coating	Minimum Aperture	Dia-phragm Blades
Macrophoto 20f3.5	1978	3, 4	S.C.	22	6
Macrophoto 35f2.8	1978	4, 6	S.S.C.	22	9
FL M 100f4	1969	3, 5		22	8
E 50f3.5	1964	3, 4		22	8

Mark What?

A glance at the online museum shows that Canon produced a prodigious number of manual focus lenses. A closer look reveals that several are near duplicates of one another. For example, Canon introduced an R50 f1.8 in 1959 with the original Canonflex. 16 months later (August 1961) Canon launched another R50 f1.8 followed by a third version in April 1963. For convenience, Canon refers to the iterations as Mark I, Mark II, and so forth.

In all, Canon produced multiple iterations of 16 manual focus SLR lenses. Figure 3.8 notes the principal iterations along with the dates on which they were introduced.[2]

Figure 3.8 Lens Iterations

	Mark I	Mark II	Mark III
R50 f1.8	May 1959	August 1960	April 1963
R100 f3.5	May 1961	April 1963	
R135 f3.5	May 1959	July 1961	
FL50 f1.4	September 1966	May 1968	
FL50 f1.8	March 1964	March 1968	
FL58 f1.2	March 1964	March 1966	
FL200 f3.5	March 1964	May 1966	
FD35 f2	March 1971	No date posted	January 1973
FD35 f2 S.S.C.	March 1973	April 1976	
FD35 f3.5 S.C.	March 1973	March 1975	July 1977
FD50 f1.4 S.S.C.	March 1973	June 1973	
FD50 f1.8	March 1971	November 1971	
FD50 f1.8 S.C.	March 1973	March 1976	
FD135 f3.5 S.C.	March 1973	November 1976	
EX35 f3.5	October 1969	No date posted	
EX125 f3.5	May 1970	August 1971	

2 The data in this table comes from Canon's online museum. Collectors have noted some errors in museum data, but none appear to affect this information.

The progressive iteration of popular lenses is well known, but its significance is not well documented. This has generated hours of discussion among both collectors and users. Some collectors view many of the iterations as inconsequential and often note that essentially the same optical designs were carried forward from one generation to the next. For example, the venerable 50mm f1.8 used an optical structure developed for screw-mount cameras and carried forward through R, FL, and FD mount versions.

Systematic analysis suggests that the progression tells us more about the evolution of Canon's manufacturing strategy than the development of new optics. The iterations are clustered among lenses at popular focal lengths and even prices remained more or less constant with significant increases in only four cases. Most changes were modest and only four involved optical groups or apertures[3] while closest focus, magnification, and filter sizes remain constant from one generation to the next.

The median time between iterations was 24 months and only one was shorter than six months. The FD50mm f1.4 S.S.C. (II) was released just three months after the first iteration, but the optical structure remained unchanged. Finally, the last documented iteration took place in 1976. Canon continued to introduce new lenses until it ceased producing manual focus SLRs, but none of the FDn lenses are marked as iterations.[4]

All told, the pattern suggests that Canon took advantage of manufacturing batches to make primarily modest changes and abandoned the practice of marking iterations as it refined its manufacturing process.

Collectibility

Like cameras themselves, Canon manual focus lenses are highly collectible. Prices range from under $10 for common lenses in user condition to several thousand dollars for unusual pieces in mint condition. On auction sites, common pieces occasionally remain unsold, even at reasonable prices, while competition for more desirable pieces is brisk.

---

3 Significant optical changes are evident in the FL50 f1.4(II), FD35f2 S.S.C. (II), FD35f3.5 SSC (II), and FD135f3.5 S.S.C. (II).

4 Curiously, Canon resumed the practice of marking iterations with a few EOS lenses.

As noted in the Introduction, desirability is determined by five factors: historic significance, original quality, rarity, condition, and personal interests. It is difficult to account for personal interests, but there are somewhat more objective indicators for the other factors.

Historic Significance

By the time Canon introduced its first manual focus SLRs, most key lens production issues had been resolved and several optical formulas were carried over from screw-mount rangefinder lenses. However, producing zoom lenses that matched the optical quality of prime lenses remained a challenge as was minimizing chromatic aberration and controlling perspective distortion. Canon made significant contributions on all three fronts and the resulting lenses may be considered historically significant.

- Introduced in 1963, the R55-135f3.5 was Canon's first zoom lens and the design carried forward with the FL55-135f3.5. Two other Canon zooms made their first appearance with the FL line: FL100-200f5.6 and FL85-300f5.

- In 1969 Canon introduced the FL-F 300f5.6 with elements containing artificially grown fluorite crystals. The use of low dispersion fluorite elements substantially reduces chromatic aberation and gave Canon a substantial advantage in producing super telephoto lenses.

- In 1971, Canon introduced the world's first 35mm interchangeable lens with an aspherical element, the FD55f1.2AL. The lens also incorporates Canon's first use of their floating element design and both features reappeared in 1976 with the FD85f1.2 S.S.C. Aspherical.

- In 1973, Canon introduced the TS 35f2.8 S.S.C, the world's first wide angle tilt and shift lens for 35mm SLR cameras. The TS mechanism allows photographers to change the relationship between the film plane and the lens' optical axis to control perspective distortion and/or modify the apparent depth of field.

Original Quality

Canon's best lenses are competitive with the finest interchangeable lenses produced by any manufacturer. Many feature large maximum apertures, special glass elements and coatings, finer tolerances and closer inspection than consumer grade lenses of comparable focal lengths. The "AL" designation distinguished several as does the "Fluorite" mark and Canon reserved Super Spectra Coating (S.S.C.) for its best lenses.

In 1978 Canon replaced other special designations with L (for "luxury") to mark its premium lenses. L lenses are very collectible as are earlier lenses with premium designations.

While Canon has a well deserved reputation for lens quality, the company has produced a handful of inferior lenses. They are less desirable and many collectors shun the FD/FDn 100-200f5.6 and FDn 100-300f5.6.

The FDn 50f2 is a special case that demonstrates criteria occasionally conflict with one another. The lens is a cheapened version of the 50f1.8 manufactured by Cosina for the T60. Relatively few were made and its relative rarity makes it a desirable collectible in spite of its inferior quality.

Rarity

Canon has never released production figures and collectors make judgments of rarity based on their own experiences. As you search for lenses, you may see expressions that reflect other collectors' experiences. "Uber rare" generally means "I have never seen one" while "rare" can be translated as "I have one but my friends don't." "Moderately rare" usually means something like "my friends and I have a couple, but few other people do" while "common" can be translated as "everyone has one, don't they?"

These "seat of the pants" judgments raise as many questions as they answer. Sadly, calculating more refined measures is a daunting task. A handful of collectors has compared serial numbers on FDn 85f2.8 Soft Focus lenses and concluded that Canon made approximately 2500 pieces. However the task consumed so much effort that no one has repeated it with other lenses.[5]

---

5   Thanks to Mark Wahlster on the FD Forum, December 1, 2010, for this reference. For details, see the thread at http://photo.net/canon-fd-camera-forum/00XoRQ.

Another approach is to take grab samples of lenses offered for sale on eBay or in other venues. It is a time consuming task and numerous extraneous factors can affect the results. Nevertheless, several grabs of between 200 and 500 lenses reveals a general pattern summarized in the following bullet points:

- FL lenses outnumber R and Canonmatic lenses by around 20 to 1
- FD/FDn lenses outnumber FL lenses by approximately 5 to 1
- Three lenses account for slightly more than half of all FD/FDn lenses available: 50f1.8, 50f1.4, and 28f2.8. The seemingly ubiquitous 70-210f4 is a distant fourth with under 5% of the lenses sampled.

The pattern reflects the popularity of Canon cameras, especially the AE-1. The FD 50 lenses were "kit" and "upgrade" lenses for the AE-1 while the 28f2.8 and 70-210f4 were relatively inexpensive additions to amateur photographers' kits.

Condition

The final consideration is condition. Fine distinctions are problematic (remember, "condition is in the eye of the beholder"), but broad distinctions between mint and lesser grades are useful. Lenses with fewer signs of wear, use, and abuse are more desirable than worn pieces.[6]

The Balancing Act

Collectors balance the five factors every time they consider adding a lens to their collections. In practice, most collectors look for lenses at the extremes: large maximum apertures, extremely long and short focal lengths, and use of exotic materials and/or aspherical elements. Lenses with these characteristics were produced in smaller numbers and sold at higher prices than more common consumer grade lenses. As a result, there are fewer of them in the marketplace and those in near mint condition are exceedingly desirable.

You alone can decide how closely you follow the practices of other collectors. Whatever you decide, you should be aware of significant anomalies affecting price and availability of Canon manual focus lenses.

---

6 See the Appendix for a more thorough discussion of grades and grading.

Marketplace Anomalies

Supply and demand rule most collectible marketplaces. Selling prices go up when more buyers compete for items and go down when there are fewer buyers or more items. The same principles apply to the market for Canon manual focus SLR lenses, but there are a couple atypical factors driving prices.

Some items are thinly traded and it is difficult to establish a fair market value. When they do come to market, competition between two or more well-heeled collectors can drive prices to extraordinary heights. Simultaneously, sellers may set reserve prices that exceed potential buyers' expectations. For example, a collector recently offered four long FL lenses for sale on eBay. The lenses attracted 40 bids, but only one sold; an FL-F 500f5.6 that went for over one thousand dollars. The other three—an FL 1200 head unit, an FL 600f5.6 with focusing unit and an FL 800f8 with focusing unit—attracted a total of 29 bids, but did not sell because the seller's reserve was not met.

Another anomaly arises from competition between users and collectors. With relatively inexpensive adapters, users can mount Canon manual focus lenses on a variety of other film and digital cameras. Readily available adapters can mate FL and FD/FDn lenses to Canon EOS cameras as well as Leica, Nikon, Panasonic, Sony/Minolta, micro 4/3, Olympus, and Pentax bodies. As a result, Canon manual focus lenses are attractive alternatives to more expensive new manufacturer and third-party lenses. In addition, a new generation of users is warming to manual focus film photography. The quality of Canon lenses is widely recognized and demand for even common lenses has grown substantially. User lenses often sell for more than collectibility alone would justify. Prices for Canon manual focus 35f2, 50f1.8, 50f1.4, and 55f1.2 lenses have benefited most from this phenomenon.

Finally, another factor is at play as well. Sensors in many digital cameras are smaller than the standard 24x36mm film frame. The image circles projected by Canon manual focus lenses extend beyond the boundaries of many digital image sensors and artificially reduce angles of view. For example, the sensor on my Canon 450D captures an area 14.8 by 22.2mm, approximately 2/3 the size of the film frame. The result is a "crop factor" of 1.6. Consequently, 28mm lenses are equivalent to standard lenses and 50mm standard lenses function as if they were modest telephotos of 80mm.

Similar crop factors arise with all but full frame digital cameras[7] and demand for short lenses has grown faster than otherwise expected. Canon manual focus SLR lenses of 17mm, 19mm, 20mm, 24mm, and even 35mm are in demand and buyers are also driving up prices for much rarer fish eye lenses.

Coincidentally, the crop factor makes it difficult to use longer lenses on many digital cameras. For example, with my 450D and a crop factor of 1.6, 200mm lenses have the same angle of view as 320mm telephotos and few photographers can use them effectively without a tripod. As a result, most shooters prefer modern image stabilized long lenses and users are a tiny fraction of the market for long lenses.

Conclusion

Canon manual focus SLR lenses are highly collectible and this chapter has covered the background you need to make informed selections. A handful of third party books published during the 1960s and 1970s offer additional details, but Canon user guides are the best source of reliable information.

Beyond bodies and lenses, Canon accessories are also desirable additions to many collections. The next chapter describes many of the most important.

---

7 For a nice summary of comparable figures on other cameras and sensor sizes, see http://en.wikipedia.org/wiki/Image_sensor_format.

Chapter 4: Canon Manual Focus Accessories

Collectors have yet to show as much interest in Canon manual focus accessories as in bodies and lenses. Neither a microphoto coupler, for example, nor a J-3 Flash Unit is as "sexy" as an F-1 body or a 20mm lens.

Although they are less glamorous, accessories deserve a prominent place in any substantial Canon collection. Many of Canon's greatest manual focus SLRs depend on accessories to achieve their full potentials. For example, the first two generations of F-1 cameras have only manual exposure. Accessories add both shutter and aperture priority modes as well as automatic film advance and remote shooting. External flashes, motor drives, meters, boosters, and other accessories make up for what some now see as "limitations."

In addition, including accessories in your collection makes it possible to recreate classic kits. In the 1960s, for example, a well-developed FX kit included the body, three or four FL lenses, a meter booster, various filters, and a J-2 or J-3 flash unit. A decade later, an FTb kit probably featured several FD lenses as well as close up lenses or extension tubes, a 133D Speed-lite, a dioptric adjustment lens and magnifier plus an angle finder.

Finally, collecting accessories presents great buying opportunities for knowledgeable collectors. While rare bodies and uncommon lenses command premium prices, accessories that were originally prized by users languish. Others are "tossed in" or added to kits to sweeten deals for cameras. Nearly half of the accessories in my collection were free and I bought many others for pennies, literally–just 99 cents for a mint V-3 flash unit with case. Other interesting pieces came to me from sellers who advertised "I don't know what it is, but it looks brand new."

Unfortunately, it is much harder to find reliable information about many accessories. Canon's online museum has page-length information about each manual focus body and nearly as much information about most R, FL, FD, and FDn lenses. Curiously, there is not a single page about accessories.

Like many other collectors, I've gathered information from web sites and aftermarket books, but some of the details are suspect. For more reliable information, I've turned to original Canon instruction sheets and product guides. The process has been laborious and the sources are increasingly difficult to find. This chapter will save you much of the bother.

Dating Canon accessories is even more difficult. Production codes described in the first chapter can be used to date some pieces, but a comprehensive survey would be required to determine when particular accessories were introduced and how long they stayed in production. Conducting such a survey would be a daunting task and I've used a shortcut that generates reasonable approximations. In my research notes, I've recorded the earliest camera users' manual that refers to each accessory. I realize that the process introduces some modest errors, but Canon introduced new bodies so frequently that my approximations are probably off by no more than a year or two.

This chapter summarizes the principal accessories used with Canon manual focus SLRs. It begins with meters and meter boosters, and moves on to flash units, motor drives, macro/micro accessories, screens, eye piece adjustment lenses (diopters), and data backs. The final section describes some other accessories designed specifically for the F-1 family.

Meters and Meter Boosters

The first three Canonflex bodies lacked built-in meters as did the FP. Photographers of the era did not mind because most used hand-held exposure meters. Prominent manufacturers included Weston, General Electric, Gossen, Walz, and Dejur-Amsco.

Canon added to the supply by offering its own meters. Many look a great deal like clip-on meters for the company's popular rangefinder cameras, but Canon produced dedicated meters for the Canonflexes as well as the FP. The company also produced a booster for FL mount bodies along with a booster finder for the original F-1.

The Canon Meter R uses a selenium cell and mounts in a shoe on the front of the body. A serrated cog wheel atop the meter engages serrations on the shutter speed dial. Meter R features both ASA (6-3200) and DIN film speed calibrations and separate indices for high and low sensitivity as well as an incident light attachment. Shutter speeds range from 8 seconds to 1/1000 second. A much scarcer second version extends shutter speeds to 1/2000.

The FP meter slips into the accessory shoe atop the pentaprism and mates with the shutter speed dial. Using a CdS cell, the meter has high and low settings and reads light from EV1 to 18. Film speeds can be set for ASA (100 to 800) or DIN (11-30) and shutter speeds range from 1 second to 1/1000 second plus B and X. It is powered by a 1.3 volt mercury battery and recognizes apertures from 1 to 22.

Figure 4.1 Pellix QL with Booster

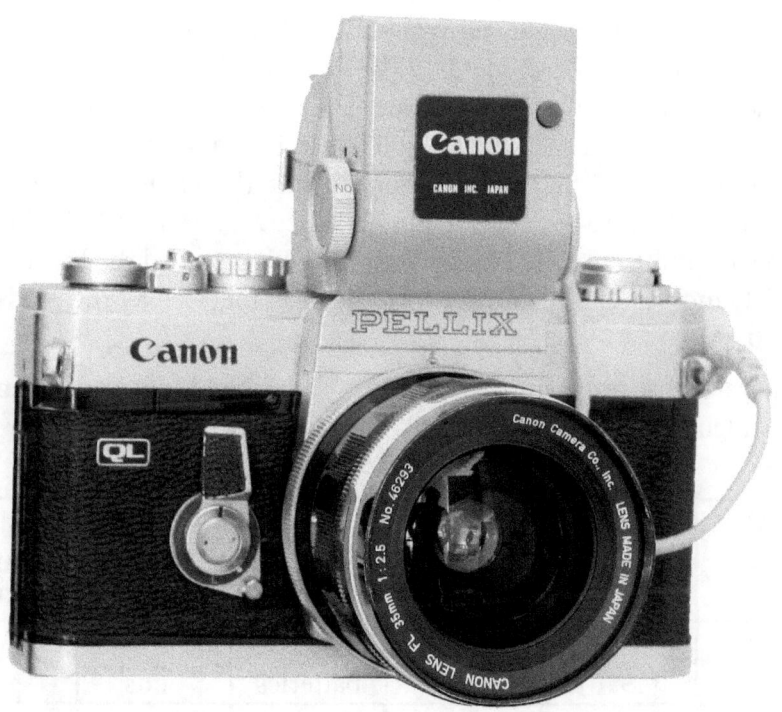

Introduced with the Pellix QL, the Canon Booster mounts in the accessory shoe and connects electronically via a short cable permanently affixed to the booster. Using a CdS cell powered by two 1.3 volt mercury batteries, the booster recognizes film speeds from ASA 25 to 12,800 and extends the metering range to EV -4.5 to 18. A second version introduced with the FTb has a modified shoe mount but is otherwise identical to the first.

All five of these items are highly collectible, but seldom used. Canon-flex and FP meters are relatively rare while boosters show up regularly. Remarkably, many boosters are in superb condition and I suspect few were used regularly.

In addition to the meters and booster described here, Canon offered a more specialized booster/finder for the original F-1. It is described among the F-1 accessories at the end of this chapter.

Flash Units and Speedlites

Canonflex bodies employed flash units originally developed for use on rangefinder cameras. Flash units J-2, J-3, V-2 and V-3 are mentioned in early user manuals and product guides. The first Speedlites including the 100 and 200 appeared with the FX and Speedlite 100S made its first appearance with the Pellix. The 102 was launched with the TL. By 1976, Speedlites 011A, 133D 155A, 166A, 188A, 199A, 277T, 299T, 533G, and 577G were available for the AE-1. The Macro Auto Ring Light joined the line up with the AV-1, and the 244T came out with the T-50 followed by the 300TL with the T-90.

Figure 4.2 lists the primary Speedlites developed for use with Canon manual focus SLRs.[1]

Figure 4.2 Canon Speedlites

Speedlite	Intro-duced with	Guide Number (ASA 100)	Power Sources	Recycle Time (on auto)	Also Compat-ible With
011A	AE-1 (1976)	14	Two AA batteries	0.5-9 seconds	
100	FX (1964)				
100S	Pellix (1965)				

1 Empty cells are points at which I lacked reliable informtion. If you can help fill in the blanks, pleased email me (ewskopec@yahoo.com) and I'll update the table in a new edition.

Speedlite	Intro-duced with	Guide Number (ASA 100)	Power Sources	Recycle Time (on auto)	Also Compat-ible With
102	TL (1967)				
133A	AV-1 (1979)	16	Four AA batteries	0.5-9 sec.	
133D	FTb (1971)	14	Four AA batteries		
155A	AT-1 (1976)	17	Four AA batteries	0.5-7 sec.	
166A	AE-1 (1976)	20	Four AA batteries	0.5-7 sec.	
177A	AE-1 (1976)	25	Four AA batteries	.5-8 sec.	
188A	AE-1 (1976)	25	Four AA batteries	0.5-8 sec	
199A	AT-1 (1976)	30	Four AA batteries	0.2-10 sec.	
200	FX (1964)				
244T	T50 (1983)	16	Two AA batteries	9 seconds or less	All FD-mount cameras
277T	A-1 (1978)	25	Four AA batteries	.5-8sec	
299T	A-1 (1978)	30	Four AA batteries	.2-13 seconds	T-series, A-series, and F-1 cameras
300TL	T90 (1986)	25-40*	Four AA batteries.	0.2 to 13 secs.	

Speedlite	Intro-duced with	Guide Number (ASA 100)	Power Sources	Recycle Time (on auto)	Also Compat-ible With
500A	Collectors are unsure if Canon ever produced Speedlite 500A. Bob Shell describes it as a hammer-head flash designed to work with the CAT system. Some printings of the original F-1 *Instructions* apparently mention it, but mine do not.				
533G	A-1 (1978)	36	Six AA batteries or external Transistor Pack G with 6 C batteries	0.2-10 sec. with	A- and T-series cameras.
577G	AE-1P (1981)	48	6 C-size batteries or Ni-Cd Pack TP in the Transistor Pack G	0.2-18 sec.	A- and T-series cameras.
ML-1	AL-1 (1982)	16	Eight AA batteries	~4 seconds	A- and T-series cameras.
ML-2	T90 (1986)	11/5.6**	Four AA batteries	0.2-13 seconds	A or T series SLRs but loses TTL capacity

*The variable guide number for the 300TL reflects settings for 24, 35, 50, and 85mm lenses.
**The ML-2 has high and low power settings.

Photographers of the era were accustomed to calculating flash expo-sure, but Canon made a short-lived effort to automate the process. Dubbed Canon Auto Tuning (CAT), the system relied on lens focus distance to cal-culate the exposure. Flash Auto Rings attached to selected lenses equipped with external pins. Turning the lens focusing ring causes the pin to press on a lever attached to the Auto Ring which then communicates focusing distance to Speedlite 133D which determines the correct exposure.

Figure 4.3 identifies the four lenses equipped with the requisite pin and appropriate Flash Auto Ring.

Figure 4.3 Canon Flash Auto Rings

Lens	Flash Auto Ring
FD 50f1.8	A2 or A
FD 50f1.4	B2 or B
FD 35f2	A, A2, B, or B2
FD 35f3.5	A2 or B2

Motor Drives and Power Winders

Automatic film advance was a major step forward in the 1970s. User convenience was a primary selling point, but motor drives also facilitated action photography as well as remote and automated interval shooting.

For Canon, powered film advance began with the Motor Drive Unit (MDU) introduced with the F-1 in 1971. The MDU is an ungainly unit and has a vertical handle that screws into the base of the camera plus an exter-nal battery pack. Canon soon replaced the MDU with the MF Motordrive. As a result, the original MDUs are highly collectible but seldom used.

The MDU and MF Motor Drive are compatible only with the F-1, but Canon anticipated a broader market. The company introduced the Power Winder A with the AT-1 and the Power Winder A2 with the AE-1. Two years later, the Motor Drive MA with its Battery Pack MA joined the lineup with the A-1 and a Ni-Cd battery pack was subsequently released with the AE-1 Program. The AE Motor Drive FN and AE Power Winder FN were released with the New F-1. Thereafter, all of the T series cameras except the T60 had built in winders.

Figure 4.4 summarizes the principal power winders available from Canon.[2]

Figure 4.4 Canon Power Winders and Drives[3]

Drive	Intro- duced With	Power Sources	Maximum Frames per Second	Also Com- patible With
MDU	F-1 (1971)	Ten AA batteries	3	None
MF Motor Drive	F-1 (1971)	Ten AA batteries	3.6	F-1n
Power Winder A	AT-1 (1976)	Four AA batter- ies	2	All A-series bodies
Motor Drive MA	A-1 (1978)	Twelve AA bat- teries.	4 or 5 fps with NiCad battery pack	AE-1 Pro- gram
Power Winder A 2	AE-1 Program (1981)	Four AA batter- ies	2	All A-series bodies
AE Motor Drive FN	New F-1 (1981)	Six AA Batter- ies or optional power sources, including the High Power Ni- Cd Pack FN	3.5 or 5 fps	None
AE Power Winder FN	New F-1 (1981)	Six AA batteries, NiCd Pack FN or High Power Ni-Cd Pack FN with built-in Ni- Cd batteries.	5 fps	None

2 Other companies produced motor drives compatible with selected Canon cameras. I've used a few that are quite capable, but none are as collectible as the Canon drives and they are not covered here.

3 In Canon's lexicon, "drives" have vertical shutter release buttons that "winders" lack.

Motor drives also support remote or interval shooting with selected bodies. Power Winder A2 and Motor Drive MA permitted the use of Wireless Controller LC-1 and Interval Timer TM-1 Quartz with the A1 and AE-1P. AE Motor Drive FN and AE Power Winder FN offered the same capability for the New F-1.

Wireless Controller LC-1 allows photographers to control the camera from as far as 60 meters away. The device has two components: a receiver attached to the camera and motor drive plus a hand-held transmitter. When activated, the transmitter sends an infrared signal to the receiver which fires the camera and advances the film.

The LC-1 can be set to different channels and a photographer can control as many as three cameras, each with a separate receiver from a single transmitter.

The Interval Timer TM-1 Quartz is designed for untended and time-lapse photography. It has 14 different time settings, from one shot per second to one every 30 minutes. When used with a 250 frame film back, it can fire one shot per minute for more than four hours.

Both the Wireless Controller and Interval Timer are relatively scarce. They are highly collectible, but seldom used.

Macro and Micro Accessories[4]

By the time Canon released the Canonflex RM in 1962, the company offered a substantial set of macrophotography accessories. The line-up included Bellows R, a waist level viewer (more accurately called an angle viewer), Copy stand 3R, Macrophotography Unit, and six extension tubes from 25 to 200mm.

A new angle viewer (Waist Level Viewer Model 2) appeared with the FX along with Bellows FL, two Macrophoto Couplers (FL 48 and FL 58), two FL extension tubes (FL 15 and FL 25), three M extension tubes (M 5, M 15, and M 20), and close-up lenses in 48mm and 58mm sizes.

---

4 Although the terms are not precisely defined, many photographers use "close-up" photography to refer to images from 10% to life sized. "Macro" typically describes images from life sized to about 10X life size and "micro" refers to images magnified above that level.

New 58mm close-up lenses were released with the Pellix (lenses 240, 450, 1800) along with Photomicro Unit F. Angle Finder A joined the line-up with the FT QL. Auto Bellows and Bellows M are first mentioned with the F-1 and Magnifier S with an adapter and a MacroPhoto Hood were available for the FTb in the same year.

Angle Finders A2 and B were available for the EF and two macrophoto lenses (20mm f3.5 and 35mm f2.8) are first mentioned in the TX user's manual while a focusing rail and macro stage joined the family with the AT-1. The AE-1 brought FD-U extension tubes and the Macro Auto Ring light. Two years later, the A-1 manual refers to four slide duplicators and two copy stands (Copy Stand 5 and Copy Stand 4).

Macrophoto coupler FL and macro adapter MA permit reversing lenses for extreme close-up work. Although the coupler has a focusing hellicoid, many photographers preferred more elegant solutions with extension tubes and bellows.

Figure 4.5 Canon Extension Tubes[5]

Type	Introduced With	Sizes	Comments
R	*Canonflex (1959)*	25, 50, 75, 100, 150, 200	
FL	*FX (1964)*	15, 25	
M	*FX (1964)*	5, 15, 20	M extension tubes only have lens and body mounts and lack the mechanics of later FD tubes.
FD-U	*A-1 (1978)*	15, 25, 50	The FD-U extension tubes are auto aperture tubes.
Vari	*F-1 (1971)*	15-25, 30-55	The Vari extension tubes feature abjustable length, but manual aperture control is necessary.

5 Blank cells mark points at which I lacked reliable data. In addition, I've used italics for attributions about which I am uncertain.

Bellows are more specialized macrophoto accessories. Whereas the effective length of stacked extension tubes is limited by the mechanics of supporting a lens at a distance from the camera body, Canon bellows allow extensions of up to 175mm and more precise control of the distance between the lens and the film plane. Figure 4.6 summarizes the principal Canon bellows.

Figure 4.6 Canon Bellows Units

Type	Introduced With	Extension Range	Comments
R	*Canonflex (1959)*	- 125mm	Bellows R does double duty. In addition to macro photography, it serves as a focusing unit for 300mm and longer lenses.
FL	FX (1964)	35-150	Bellows FL maintains the automatic diaphragm control of a normally mounted FD or FL lens and has a built-in focusing rail, but it lacks the camera flipping capabilities of the Autobellows.
Auto-bellows	F-1 (1971)	39-175mm	The Autobellows is the most sophisticated model with a built-in focusing rail. It allows flipping the camera to horizontal and vertical positions and uses a double cable release for full aperture focusing. However it does not support full aperture metering.
M	F-1 (1971)	-	Bellows M is the least complex model. It is similar to the Autobellows but lacks a focusing rail and does not have camera flipping capability.

Focusing Screens

Beginning with the F-1 Canon offered interchangeable focusing screens for selected bodies. Aside from the A-1, they are user changeable.

Beginning with the F-1, Canon uses alphabetic designations for specific screens. Four are available for the original F-1 and the number grows to thirteen designated A through M with New F-1. Typical screens have rangefinder spots in the center of matte fields (screens A, B, and E), all-matte screens with matte-only circles in the center (screen C), and screens with double cross hairs in clear center spots (screen I). More specialized screens are optimized for slow lenses (screen G) and fast lenses (screen F) as well as screens with grids (screen D), horizontal and vertical scales (screen H), and cross split images (screen L).

As Canon expanded the number of available screens, the company did not "back fill" offerings for earlier bodies. Figure 4.7 summarizes available screens for selected bodies.

Figure 4.7 Interchangeable Focusing Screens

	F-1	F-1n	A-1	AE-1P	New F-1	T90
A	✓	✓	✓	✓	✓	✓
B	✓	✓	✓	✓	✓	✓
C	✓	✓	✓	✓	✓	✓
D	✓	✓	✓	✓	✓	✓
E		✓	✓		✓	
F		✓			✓	
G		✓	✓		✓	
H		✓		✓	✓	✓
I		✓	✓	✓	✓	✓
J					✓	
K					✓	
L				✓	✓	✓
M					✓	

With the New F-1, Canon incorporated metering patterns in the focusing screens. All F-1N focusing screens are called FN screens and carry two letter designations. The second letter identifies the specific screen while the first indicates the supported metering pattern. "A" denotes center weighted averaging, "P" indicates partial metering on the central 12%, and "S" is Spot metering on a 3% center spot. For example, screen PH provides partial center weighted metering on a 12% circle (that's the P) on a matte screen with horizontal and vertical scales (that's the H).

All 13 types are available for both center-weighted average and selective-area metering, but only six types (screens B, C, E, I, J and K) are available for spot metering. As a result, Canon offered a total of 32 FN screens for the New F-1.

Canon focusing screens come to market regularly including unused items in their original boxes. They are only modestly collectible but specific screens may be difficult to find. Prices remain modest (on the order of $15), but F-1N screens may sell for significantly higher prices. I suspect higher prices for the New F-1 screens are driven by users competing for the most desirable items.

Dioptric Adjustment Lenses

Eyesight adjustment lenses attach to the rear of the viewfinder eyepiece and simplify photography for people who normally wear glasses. Canon introduced four with the FX and increased the number to ten with the TLb. The company typically refers to them as Dioptric Adjustment Lenses, but occasionally calls them "diopters" or "copters."

Few camera *Instructions* mention them all, but Canon produced dioptric adjustment lenses from -4 to +3 in both square and round forms.[6] Type R diopters are round and screw into the back of round F-1 viewfinder eyepieces.

Type S diopters are square and slip onto matching viewfinder eyepieces. They fit virtually all Canon manual focus SLRs other than the F-1s. Both round and square diopters are relatively common although pieces with specific values may be difficult to find and prices under $20 are common.

---

6   The actual values are -4, -3, -2, -0.5, 0, +.5, +1, +1.5, +2, and +3.

Data Backs

Data backs replace standard camera backs and add the ability to record dates and other information on the lower right corner of the film frame. Data back A was introduced with the AT-1 and can be used with all A-series cameras except the AV-1. It is powered by a single 6V battery and can record dates (year, month, and day) as well as letters (A-G both upper and lower case) and Roman Numerals (1-X). Values are set by turning 3 dials on the back and the recording light intensity is set with a 3-level toggle switch.

Data back FN was introduced with the New F-1. It offers the same capabilities of back A, requires a 6V battery, and is compatible only with the F-1N.

Data backs 70, 80, and 90 fit the corresponding T-series cameras. They record the same data as earlier backs, but reflect Canon's growing mastery of microelectronic technology. All three backs are powered by 3V lithium batteries and feature LCD screens. Data values are set with button switches and an integrated calendar is programmed from 1983 to 2029. It automatically accommodates short months and leap years.

The T-series backs also add significant control features to the bodies. Functions include self timer, interval timer, long exposure mode, and frame counter setting for the number of exposures. Data Back 90 is modestly more sophisticated than either the 70 or 80. Film speed and recording light intensity are set automatically by the 90 but must be set manually on the other two.

In addition, Canon offered a more sophisticated back for the T90 capable of transfering data to a personal computer. Called the Data Memory Back 90, it was available only in selected markets. It can record 16 shot variables for up to 156 exposures or six variables for up to 338 exposures. As offered, the back supported only the MSX home computer standard but third parties have adapted connectors for other interfaces.

F-1 Specific Accessories

The F-1 was the flagship of the Canon line. When it was released in 1971, Canon maintained that the F-1 offered more accessories than any other camera. In the *Instructions*, Canon gave top billing to four: the Booster T Finder, Servo EE Finder, Motor Drive Unit, and Film Chamber 250. Subsequent pages mention four Focusing Screens, eight screw-in dioptric adjustment lenses, Angle Finder B, the Canon Magnifier, an Eyecup, Flash V-3, Speedlite 133D, Flash Couplers L and D, the Flash Auto Ring, various filters, and interchangeable lenses. Near the end of the manual, Canon presents a full page of accessories, most of which are shared with other bodies.

Instructions for the F-1n follow the same pattern and highlight Motor Drive MF, the Servo EE finder, Booster T Finder, and Film Chamber 250. Subsequent pages mention nine focusing screens, ten Dioptric Adjustment Lenses, Angle Finders A2 and B, Magnifier R, Eye Cup R, Speedlite 133D, Flash Couplers L and D, Flash Auto Rings A2 and B2, and various filters. New items include a Battery Case and Magazines 15V and 12V plus cords as well as Film Loader 250 and Film Magazine 250. Canon also included a full page of "Close-up, Macrophotography, and Photomicrography" accessories.

Instructions for the New F-1 are nearly as long as those for the first two F-1s combined. The additional pages detail the new focusing screens, use of seven Speedlites, and shooting with close-up accessories. The final pages describe key "system accessories," including the AE Motor Drive FN, AE Power Winder FN, Film Chamber FN-100, Data Back FN, and Wireless Controller LC-1.

From the start, Canon conceptualized the F-1 as the heart of a complete photographic system. Lenses and flash units could be used with other bodies, but Canon also produced accessories that are exclusive to the F-1.

Viewfinders are among the most important F-1 accessories. They allow photographers to view subjects in their preferred manner and add some exposure modes not provided by the bodies themselves.

Figure 4.7 summarizes viewfinders for the F-1/F-1n and New F-1.

Figure 4.7 F-1 Viewfinders[7]

F-1 and F-1n	Eye-Level Finder is the standard finder originally shipped with the body. Like other finders for the F-1 and F-1n, it lacks a hotshoe and Canon sold three separate flash adapters described below.
	Waist-Level Finder is patterned after those on common medium format cameras. Users view their subjects by looking straight down into the finder which features a pop-up screen to eliminate stray light and a 5X magnifier to help with critical focusing. Metering information is not visible through the waist level finder.
	Speed Finder is unique to the F-1 system and allows users to see the viewfinder image from two and a half inches (60mm) away. It swivels between eye-level and waist-level configurations.
	Booster T Finder adds an ultra sensitive metering cell reading as low as EV -3.5. It also adds electronic timing for long exposures.
	Servo EE Finder adds shutter priority AE with a servo mechanism to stop the lens down to shooting aperture. It requires an external power source such as a battery magazine with 8 AA batteries or motor drive MF.
F-1 N	Eye -Level Finder FN is similar to the original eye level finder, but adds a hot shoe and integral eyepiece shutter.
	AE Finder FN has a hot shoe and integral eyepiece shutter. It also offers aperture-priority AE and supports shutter-priority AE when a power drive is attached.
	Like the original, Speed Finder FN switches between eye-level and waist-level viewing and images are visible up to two and a half inches (60mm) away. It adds a hot shoe to the original configuration.
	Waist-Level Finder FN is a twin of the original, but modified to fit the New F-1.
	Waist-Level Finder FN-6X is similar to the original waist-level finder and waist-level finder FN, but increases magnification to 6X and has an internal stepless diopter adjustment from -5 to +3.

7 Viewfinders for the New F-1 are similar to earlier models but are not compatible with the original F-1 or F-1n. The new models add an "FN" designation.

Finders for the F-1 and F-1n lacked hot shoes and Canon offered three accessory couplers. Flash Coupler D slides over the rewind knob and supports X-sync flash for nondedicated flash units. Flash Coupler L also mounts over the rewind knob and adds support for Canon's CAT system.

Flash Coupler F clips over the eye-level finder with a pair of prongs that engage the contacts either side of the rewind knob and a fixing ring that attaches to the eyepiece. It does not work well with other viewfinders and does not support the CAT System.

Both collectors and users recognize the value of F-1 viewfinders and market prices are climbing. The three flash couplers are relatively rare and I have witnessed too few transactions to suggest meaningful prices. Other experienced collectors report that the D is most common while the F is the rarest model.

The F-1 retained its perch atop the line until Canon released the EOS-1 in 1989. Many accessories produced during the F-1's 18-year reign are available at generally reasonable prices. Nevertheless, collectors need to exercise care because most accessories for the F-1 and F-1n are not fully compatible with those made for the New F-1 and vice versa.

Conclusion

Throughout the manual focus era, Canon offered a broad range of accessories. Canon produced virtually everything a photographer might want except film. As a result, the marketplace is home to an incredible variety of accessories bearing the company's name. In addition to the items described in this chapter, the list includes gadget bags, tripod adapters, filters, cable releases, camera holders, lens mount converters, and lens hoods. The vast majority appear to be authentic and market prices have yet to reach levels required to make counterfeiting profitable.

Collectors have been relatively slow to recognize the value of accessories and many are undervalued. As a result, it is still possible to build substantial collections and recreate classic kits. However, demand is growing as more collectors and some users compete for the most desirable pieces.

Chapter 5: Third-Party Lenses

As Canon cameras became popular, other manufacturers and distributors sold lenses to fit. Names you may see include Vivitar, Soligor, Spiratone, Panagor, Tamron, Sigma, and Tokina. In addition, retailers often sold lenses under their own names and both Sears and JC Penny lenses show up frequently.

Many third-party lenses targeted cost-conscious consumers. They were designed to be "serviceable" and inexpensive. Others extended the Canon line by adding focal lengths and other features. A few actually outperformed their Canon equivalents. These top-notch lenses are often called "cult classics" and some of these 40-year old lenses compare favorably to modern lenses.

"Buyer beware" is good advice when you shop for third-party lenses. Many were poorly designed and cheaply made. Even those that pass the inspection described in the Appendix are mediocre performers, at best. They are shunned by knowledgeable collectors and are best suited for careers as paper weights or door stops.

Confusion between manufacturer and distributor names is another problem. For example, Vivitar is among the most storied names in photography. Yet even in its heyday, Vivitar was a distributor and bought lenses from other manufacturers. Early Series 1 lenses manufactured by Kino Precision, Komine, and Tokina are very desirable and command premium prices. Many knowledgeable collectors avoid later pieces made by other companies.

In spite of these complications, some third-party lenses are highly collectible. In general, collectors look for high quality lenses with interesting stories confirmed by authoritative information. Coincidentally, interests of collectors and users diverge on the second and third criteria. With appropriate adaptors, R, FL, and FD mount lenses can be used on modern digital cameras. Users regularly report good experiences with lenses of little interest to collectors. For example, I regularly use a 24mm lens marked Toyo Optics on my Canon 450D, but it has no place in my collection.

To identify collectible third party lenses, you need to know a bit about manufacturers, distributors and trade or brand names. This chapter begins with Vivitar, a company that created more than its share of cult classics as well as many less desirable lenses and accessories. The remaining pages present an alphabetical list of other names you may encounter.

Vivitar

Vivitar was founded in 1938 by two German immigrants, Max Ponder and John Best. They imported German-made photographic equipment until World War II and switched to Japanese imports after the war. In the 1960s, Ponder and Best created the Vivitar brand to compete with major lens makers.

Through the early 1970s, Vivitar had its own design facilities and collaborated with Opcon Associates to create some extraordinary lenses. Manufactured by Kino Precision in Japan, Vivitar's early Series 1 lenses were as good as the best Canon, Nikon, and Zuiko lenses. Unfortunately, the lenses were just as expensive and sales were disappointing. Eventually, the company closed its design facilities and began sourcing lenses from less expensive manufacturers. The company and brand name were subsequently sold to Syntax-Brillian Corporation and then Sakar after Syntax-Brillian declared bankruptcy in 2008.

Today, Vivitar distributes inexpensive cameras, lenses, and accessories. In the words of one knowledgeable commentator, "Vivitar is a ghost of its former self, and the Series 1 name is just a trademark they slap on whatever they feel like putting it on." The story is a sad one, but collectors seek the early Series 1 lenses and consider many to be comparable to the best made today.

Vivitar's flowering lasted just a decade or so. In that time, the company designed and distributed a remarkable number of highly collectible lenses. Many are justly regarded as cult classics and Figure 5.2 lists the most desirable.

Coincidentally, from the early 1970s through about 1990, Vivitar used coded serial numbers to identify lens manufacturers. Lenses with serial numbers beginning with 6 or 9 were produced by Olympus and Cosina respectively. Two digit codes include 13 for Schneider Optik, 22 for Kino Precision, 28 for Komine Co. Ltd, 33 for Asanuma, 37 for Tokina, 42 for Bauer, 44 for Perkin Elmer, and 75 for Hoya Optical. The serial numbers also indicate the week and year of production.[1]

Figure 5.2 Highly Collectible Vivitar Lenses[2]

Series 1 28f1.9	Still considered a "fast" lens, this lens is praised for its quality and low distortion. It was expensive, heavy and not very popular in its time. Today, it is considered a cult classic.
Series 1 28-90f2.8-3.5	Covering the most popular focal lengths, this highly sought after lens uses a varifocal design to reduce size, weight and cost.
Series 1 35f1.9	This prized lens is virtually distortion-free and not prone to flare. However, radioactive elements in many pieces have turned amber over time.
Series 1 35-85f2.8	Like the Series 1 28-90, this is a varifocal lens praised for sharpness throughout its range.
70-150 f3.8 one touch	Vivitar distributed at least five models of this zoom lens. Early ones produced by Kino Precision have serial numbers beginning with 22 and are the most sought after. Users and collectors praise them for smooth, well damped motions as well as excellent resolution and color, low flare, very good contrast. Matched teleconverters produced by Kino Precision extend the focal lengths and produce noticeably better results than other multipliers.

1 Several websites explain how to interpret these codes and name manufacturers other than the better known ones mentioned here. For example, see http://www.flickr.com/groups/730208@N24/, http://www.robertstech.com/vivitar.htm, and http://www.cameraquest.com/VivLensManuf.htm.

2 Several of the lenses in this table use "varifocal" designs. They are not true zoom lenses because users must refocus after changing focal lengths. This helped to reduce size and weight while avoiding some compromises in early zoom lenses.

Series 1 90f2.5 Macro	This short telephoto macro lens remains popular in the used marketplace and is praised for its sharpness and flatness of field. Its original street price was noticeably lower than comparable but less capable lenses and it offers greater working space that more common 50mm and 55mm macro lenses.
Series 1 90-180 Flat Field Macro Zoom	Originally was designed as a medical lens, this varifocal lens was also popular among nature photographers who wanted to put some distance between themselves and dangerous or skittish subjects.
Series 1 70-210 f3.5	The Series 1 70-210 was one of Vivitar's most popular lenses and the company distributed at least six versions. The final three versions are not highly regarded, but the first three are considered classics. Buyers should look for the 1974 f3.5 edition by Kino Precision (serial numbers beginning with 22), the 1982 f3.5 edition by Tokina (serial numbers beginning with 37), or the 1984 f2.8-4 macro by Komine (serial numbers beginning with 28).
Series 1 135f2.3	Described as "a compact beauty," this lens was considered to be a good compromise between heavy, expensive f2 designs and compact f2.8 lenses. Users praise it for solid construction and a close focusing distance of 5 feet.
Series 1 200f3	Originally more expensive than many faster f2.8 lenses, this lens was praised as being sharp and compact with good contrast. Its selling points include a close focusing distance of 4 feet and use of standard 72mm filters.
Series 1 450 f4.5 Mirror	A marketplace failure owing to high price, this lens uses aspherical elements to achieve high performance, compact design, and a close focusing distance of only 12 feet. Few were sold and they are rare in today's marketplace.

Series 1 600f8 Mirror	Manufactured by Perkin Elmer, this "Solid Cat" lens uses one-piece glass construction. It is compact (3.3 inches long) and super-rugged, but few are available in today's marketplace.
Series 1 800 f11 Mirror	This is another rare "Solid Cat" produced by Perkin Elmer. Like the 600f8, it is compact and rugged.

Other Third-Party Lens Manufacturers

Search eBay or visit a local camera show and you will see an incredible variety of lenses for Canon manual focus SLRs. "For" is a code word indicating that the lenses were manufactured or distributed by someone other than Canon. The following pages list about 60 third-party names and I'm sure the enumeration is not complete.

Through the manual focus era, there were probably about 10 significant optics manufacturers in Japan plus a handful in Korea, Europe, the Soviet Union and elsewhere.[3] Many sold lenses with their own names as well as large numbers that were rebranded by distributors,

For collectors, the difference between distributors and manufacturers is extraordinarily important. Even major manufacturers produced lenses on which distributors stuck their own names. In general, rebranders shopped for less expensive lenses and accepted poor designs and uneven quality.

Documentation is also a problem with rebranded lenses. Few distributors publicized their sourcing practices and most manufacturers were reluctant to compromise sales of their own brands by acknowledging lenses sold under other names. Collectors and users love to speculate and have identified a few probable sourcing relationships by comparing rebranded lenses with those carrying the manufacturers' names. Nevertheless, it is usually difficult to identify the manufacturers of rebranded lenses and the information about Vivitar serial numbers is the exception that proves the rule.

As a result, collectors typically avoid rebranded lenses and focus on original equipment manufacturer lenses as well as a handful of third-party

3 The number 10 is merely an informed guess. It may be a pretty good approximation, but I doubt there is any way to count the numerous family-owned and operated job shops.

lenses for which adequate documentation tells an interesting story. My phrase, "not highly collectible," in the following pages does not necessarily mean that a lens is substandard—although many are—but does indicate that relatively few collectors are interested.

Access

Access lenses were distributed by Magnum Optics and Research, Inc., in Denver, Colorado. They appear to be rebranded lenses from various manufacturers and are not considered highly collectible.

Actinar

Actinar was a brand name distributed by Aetna Optix. Please see the company entry for additional details.

Accura

Accura was a brand used by Sigma and distributed by Spiratone. Please see the company entries for additional details.

Aetna Optix

Aetna Optix was a distributor of photographic equipment. Active in the 1950s, the company remained in business through the early 1990s when it was acquired by Brandess-Kalt. Aetna Optix distributed lenses branded as Actinar, Coligon and Rokunar, none of which are highly collectible.

Albinar

Albinar was a one-man importer based in New Jersey. The company rebranded Japanese lenses as well as cameras, flash units, and tripods. Albinar lenses were budget-priced consumer lenses and are not considered highly collectible.

Amcam International, Inc.

Amcam International is a Northbrook, Illinois-based distributor. At one time, its lineup included photographic equipment and the company registered seven trademarks. All of them have been abandoned but collectors still encounter them: Kotaishi (dead 1985), Stabilo (1977), Dataprinz (1977), Rexatar (1977), Rexagon (1977), Datajug (1976), and Prinzdatajug (1976).

Angenieux

Angenieux is a brand used by Pierre Angenieux beginning in 1935. Based in Saint-Etienne in France, the company is known for movie production lenses, but it also introduced the world's first retro focus lens and improved zoom lens designs for photographic and movie cameras.

Other manufacturers copied Angenieux optical designs and the company itself produced a few lenses for Leica, Nikon and Canon. These rare lenses are highly collectible.

Argraph Corporation

Argraph Corporation was founded by Irving Roth in 1953 and imported Samigon lenses during the manual focus era. The company continues to distribute photographic equipment and supplies from its warehouse in Carlstadt, New Jersey.

Asanuma

Asanuma was a brand name used by Tokina. Please see the company entry for additional details.

Bell & Howell

Canon collectors know Bell & Howell for its marketing agreement with Canon. When the agreement ended, Bell & Howell marketed rebranded Japanese-made lenses under its own name. The rebranded lenses are generic lenses of little interest to collectors. Only lenses marked with the dual B&H/Canon logo are highly collectible, Canon-made lenses.

Besteye

Besteye is an expired trademark of Marukei Sangyo Company, Limited. Please see the company entry for additional details.

Bestron

Origins unknown.

Bower

Founded in 1949, the Bower Corporation is an importer of low-cost, rebranded Japanese and Korean lenses. Users report some favorable experiences, but Bower lenses for manual focus SLRs are not considered highly collectible.

Bushnell

Bushnell is an American manufacturer of binoculars, scopes, and related outdoor equipment. Marked lenses suggest they manufactured or distributed SLR lenses for a while, but other details are lacking.

Cambron

Cambron is a house brand name for lenses and accessories sold by Cambridge Camera of New York. User opinions vary widely, but Cambron manual focus lenses are not considered to be highly collectible.

Chinon

Established in 1948, Chinon Industries, Inc. was a Japanese camera components manufacturer including Prinz lenses distributed in the United States. Chinon also produced popular cameras under its own name. The company continues to develop digital cameras on behalf of Kodak which acquired it in 2004.

Coligon

Coligon was a brand name distributed by Aetna Optix. Please see the company entry for additional details.

CPC

CPC was a trademark of Combined Products Corporation. The company was incorporated in 1951 and apparently distributed rebranded photographic equipment. It is currently listed as inactive and the CPC trademark was abandoned by 1978. Other trademarks included Tempo (abandoned by 1984), Tempo Plus (1984), Glarebuster (1984), Ozunon (1982), SLR Starter Pak (1981), and CPC Phase 2 (1978). None of the company's lenses are considered highly collectible.

Cosina

Cosina Company Ltd. of Nagano, Japan began manufacturing lenses in 1959 and changed its name from Niko in 1973. Cosina produced lenses and bodies for other companies including several later Vivitar lenses and the Canon T60.

Cosina also produced lenses and SLRs under its own name and a modest number of collectors are interested in them. Nevertheless, Cosina-manufactured Canon lenses aside from the FD50f2 are not considered highly collectible.[4]

Deitz

Origins unknown.

Dejur

DeJur-Amsco was a Long Island, New York-based company founded in the 1920s. They manufactured their own enlargers and light meters for a while, but ultimately made their name distributing rebranded photographic equipment including cameras, lenses, projectors, and enlargers.

Dejur survived until 1974 and collectors have modest interest in DeJur-branded cameras. However, manual focus SLR lenses distributed by the company are not highly collectible.

Eitar

Eitar was a brand name for lenses distributed by Reeves Photo Sales, Inc. None are considered highly collectible.

Elicar

Elicar is a brand name that appears on several Komine-made lenses. Please see the company entry for additional details.

Formula 5

Formula 5 was a trademark of Interphoto Corporation. Please see the company entry for additional details.

Five Star

Five Star was a brand name used by Toyo Optics for lenses distributed in the United States. Please see the company listing for additional details.

---

4 Today, Cosnina produces bodies and lenses under contract for the "new" Voightlander as well as selected lenses for Zeiss.

Focal

Focal was a house brand for lenses distributed by K Mart. The company filed the trademark in 1968 and abandoned it in 2002, and the lenses are not considered collectible.

Gemini

Founded in 1964, Gemini imported rebranded Japanese lenses. The company ceased operations in 2004 and Gemini branded lenses are not considered highly desirable.

Hanimex

Hanimex was an Australian distributor founded by Jack Hannes after the Second World War. The name is a contraction of HANnes IMport and EXport and the company imported both European and Japanese lenses, bodies and accessories. Hannes apparently sought lowest cost providers and Hanimex lenses have a poor reputation among users. Hanimex lenses for Canon SLRs are not considered highly collectible.

Hoya

Established in 1941, Hoya is an optical glass manufacturer. Among photographers, the company is best known for its filters and its 2007 acquisition of Pentax. At various times, Hoya has produced glass for several lens manufacturers including Bronica, Mamiya, Tamron, and Tokina.

Imado

Imado appears to have been an infrequently used trademark. Some collectors have noted that lenses with the name are remarkably similar to Tokina lenses of comparable focal lengths, but further documentation is lacking.

Interphoto Corporation

The IMC division of Interphoto Corporation was a distributor of inexpensive photographic equipment. Located in Palisades Park, New Jersey, the company's trademarks included Formula 5, Lentar, and Palmatic. Palmatic was abandoned by 1980 while Formular 5 and Lentar were abandoned a year or two earlier.

JC Penney

JC Penney rebranded lenses from several manufacturers and sold them through their chain of department stores. Today, these lenses are not considered highly collectible.

Kalimar

Kalimar, Inc., was a St. Louis, Missouri based distributor of rebadged photographic equipment from Japan, Hong Kong, Taiwan, Germany and the Soviet Union. Tiffin bought the company in 1999 and Kalimar lenses are not considered highly collectible.

Kalt

Kalt Corporation distributed rebranded Japanese lenses and was acquired by Brandess Brothers in 1987. Kalt lenses are not considered highly collectible.

Kenko

Founded in 1957, Kenko is a Japanese manufacturer of photographic accessories. At various times, the company has produced filters, extension tubes, and other accessories in addition to lenses. None are highly collectible.

Kilfitt

Kilfitt lenses have a history nearly as interesting as Vivitar. Founded in 1941 by Heinz Kilfitt, the designer of the Robot camera, the company moved to Leichtenstein in 1947 and later to Munich. In 1968, Kilfitt retired and sold the factory to Frank Back who established a headquarters in Long Island, New York and operated the factory under the Zoomar name. The company was regarded as one of the most innovative German lens makers of the 1950s and 1960s, and made the world's first production 35mm zoom lens, the 36-82/2.8 Zoomar, in 1959.

The Kilfitt factory turned out four families of lenses designated KI, AN, WE, and N. The KI lenses are the most common and highly collectible lenses include the 90f 2.8 Makro-Kilar and the 300f4 Pan-Tele-Kilar as well as 500 and 1000 catadioptric Zoomatars. The company abandoned the consumer market in 1986, but continued to produce optics for military applications.

Kino Precision Optical Company

Kino Precision was one of the leading Japanese third-party lens manufacturers during the manual focus era. Many of their lenses were substantially more expensive than lenses by other third-party manufacturers and Kino lenses are less readily available than many others.

Today, Kino Precision is best known as the manufacturer of many outstanding Vivitar Series 1 lenses and the company also sold lenses under its own brand names, Panagor and Kiron.

In addition to selected Vivitar lenses, collectors speak highly of several Kino Precision lenses sold under the Kiron name. The Kiron 24f2, 28f2, and 70-150f4 lenses all have admirers and four Kiron lenses have real cult status.

- The Kiron 28-85 f2.8-3.8 Macro Zoom is a varifocal lens praised for sharpness, contrast, and limited distortion. In 1981, *Modern Photography* described it as the best lens in this focal length that they had tested.

- The Kiron 28-105 f3.2-4.5 zoom is another varifocal lens praised for its "wonderful image quality."

- The Kiron 28-210 f3.8-5.6 is considered one of the best long zoom lenses ever made. It gets high marks for its close focus distance (3.5 feet), 1 to 4 macro reproduction, and use of 72mm filters.

- The 105 f2.5 Macro was one of the last Series 1 lenses made by Kino Precision for Vivitar and the company also sold it under the Kiron name. It is considered an outstanding macro lens even by today's standards and is described as a design case where "everything just went right."

The company discontinued production of 35mm camera lenses by 1988 and subsequently merged with 'Melles Griot Japan' to form 'Kino-Melles Griot'. In 1995 the name changed to "Melles Griot Ltd." and Kino Precision became a member of CVI Melles Griot Group in 2007.

Kiron

Kiron was a brand name used by Kino Precision Optics. Please see the company entry for additional details.

Koboron

Koboron is a trademark of Marukei Sangyo Company, Limited. Please see the company entry for additional details.

Komine

Komine is a Japanese optics company now known as Nittoh Kogaku K.K. The company produced several well-regarded Vivitar lenses as well as Elicar and some Spiratone, Rokunar and Soligor lenses.

The company remains in business, but stopped marketing its lenses directly to consumers during the mid 1980s. Pristine samples are moderately collectible.

Kotaishi

Kotaishi was a trademark used by AmCam International. Please see the company entry for additional details.

Lenmar

Lenmar distributed rebranded Japanese lenses. They are not highly collectible.

Lentar

Lentar was a trademark of Interphoto Corporation. Please see the company entry for additional details.

Lester A. Dine

Lester A. Dine is a Florida-based designer and distributor of dental photographic equipment founded in 1952. The company claims to have invented the ring flash and its manual focus 105f2.8 macro lens is prized by collectors. Physical similarities suggest the lens was manufactured by Kiron and it frequently appears in Nikon and Pentax as well as Canon mounts.

Marukei Sangyo Company, Limited

Marukei Sangyo Company, Limited, is a Japanese export company. At one time, the company had four trademarks registered in the United States. Of the four, only Koborn filed in 1985 is still active. Besteye expired in 1982 while Technon and Teknon both expired in 1985. None of their lenses are considered highly collectible.

Miida

Miida was a Japanese distributor of photographic equipment. In the United States, Miida lenses were distributed by Marubeni American Corporation. They are not considered to be highly collectible.

Mitakon

This trademark was issued to Mitakon U.S.A. Inc. of Northbrook , Illinois company in June 1983. The trademark was abandoned eight years later and lenses with the mark were probably manufactured by a Japanese company which continues operations in China as Shenyang Mitacon Optical Electronic Company, Ltd. Most are budget priced lenses and are not considered highly collectible.

Novoflex

Novoflex "Follow-Focus" lenses are famous for their interchangeable lens heads, optics optimized for center sharpness, mounts that resemble gun stocks, and bellows-like adapters for various camera mounts. The company also made some excellent macro lenses for 35mm SLRs.

Today, Novoflex lenses are rare, expensive and highly collectible.

Osawa

Osawa was a Japanese manufacturer that made lenses for a variety of cameras. User opinions vary from "lousy" to "fantastic," but Osawa lenses for Canon manual focus SLRs are not highly collectible.

Ozunon

Ozunon was a trademark of the Combined Products Corporation. Please see the corporation entry for additional details.

Pacemark

Pacemark Corporation was a Japanese manufacturer of inexpensive third-party lenses. Zykkor is the most commonly encountered trademark and older photographers recall that unscrupulous merchants often substituted Zykkor lenses for more expensive ones in bait and switch promotions. Although Pacemark was a Japanese company, at least some lenses appear to have been sourced in Korea and they are not highly collectible.

Panagor

Panagor was a brand name used by Kino Precision Optics and the company entry has additional details. Today, these lenses are attracting growing collector interest.

Palmatic

Palmatic was a trademark of Interphoto Corporation. Please see the company entry for additional details.

Peleng

Peleng is a Minsk, Belarus based manufacturer of lenses in Canon, Nikon, Olympus and other mounts. Current reviews have highlighted the company's inexpensive 8mm fisheye lens, but older lenses are not considered highly collectible.

Phoenix

Phoenix is a brand name used by Samyang and the company entry has additional details. Today, these lenses are not considered to be desirable collectibles.

Polaris

Origins unknown.

Prinz

Prinz was a distributor of inexpensive photographic accessories. The brand name is associated with mass market retailer Dixon's in the United Kingdom as well as Bass Camera of Chicago and Amcam Intenational, Inc., in the United States. In addition to lenses, the Prinz name is found on cameras, enlargers, electronic flashes, print driers, bulk film loaders and other photographic products.

Chinon produced some Prinz lenses and products may have been sourced from a variety of companies. In general, Prinz lenses and accessories targeted budget-conscious consumers and they are not highly collectible.

Pro Optic

Origins unknown.

Promaster

Promaster is a brand name for lenses procured by the Photographic Research Organization, Inc., a national retail cooperative of independent camera shops. Founded in 1958, the Photographic Research Organization rebrands items from other manufacturers and recent lenses appear to have been manufactured by Tamron.

User opinions are mixed, but Promaster lenses are not considered highly collectible.

Quantaray

Quantaray is a house brand name for lenses and accessories sold by Ritz Camera. It appears that many lenses were produced by Sigma, but other manufacturers may have produced some batches.

User opinions vary widely, but Quantaray manual focus lenses are not considered to be highly collectible.

Rexatar

Rexatar was a trademark used by AmCam International. Please see the company entry for additional details.

Rexagon

Rexagon was a trademark used by AmCam International. Please see the company entry for additional details.

Ricoh

Ricoh is a Japanese company founded in 1936 as Riken Kankoshi Co., Ltd. In 1937, the company began producing optical equipment including cameras and lenses. In 1957, Ricoh established Japan's first mass-production system for cameras and was subsequently awarded the Ohkochi Memorial Production Prize. Today, the company produces digital cameras as well as printers and other office equipment. Ricoh lenses for Canon manual focus SLRs are not considered highly collectible.

Rikenon

Rikenon lenses were made by Ricoh and distributed by Braun North America. They are not considered highly collectible.

Rokinon

Origins unknown.

Rokunar

Rokunar was a brand name distributed by Aetna Optix. Please see the company entry for additional details.

Sakar

Sakar International, Inc. is a private company located in Edison, New Jersey. Founded in 1977, Sakar produces inexpensive lenses, digital cameras, chargers, batteries, filters, flashes, card readers, Web cams, iPod accessories among other things. Today, the company owns the Vivitar brand name, but none of its lenses for Canon manual focus SLRs are considered collectible.

Samigon

Samigon lenses were distributed by Argraph Corporation.

Samyang

Samyang Optics Company Limited is a Korean company founded in 1972. They manufacture lenses under their own name and have also used the Phoenix brand name for lenses imported into the United States. They have also made rebranded lenses sold under other distributors names.

In recent years, they have apparently improved lens quality to compete with Sigma, Tamron, and Tokina. During the manual focus era, however, Samyang produced inexpensive lenses that are not regarded as highly collectible.

Sears

Sears rebranded lenses from several manufacturers and sold them through their chain of stores. Today, these lenses are not highly collectible.

Sigma

Sigma Corporation is a Japanese company founded in 1961 to manufacture lenses and other photographic accessories. The company is best known for making some of the earliest fish eye and ultrawide lenses sold under their own name as well as under brand names including Spiratone, Cambron, Accura, and Vivitar.

Many of their early lenses used T-mounts so they could be fitted to a variety of cameras. However, their lenses from the 1960s and 1970s appealed primarily to cost-conscious consumers and many were substantially below the optical quality of the era. Nevertheless, Sigma prices were attractive, especially for fish eye lenses sold under the Accura and Spiratone brand names.

In the mid-1970s, Sigma began to upgrade the quality of its optics, culminating in a higher quality series designated by the letters Z, WQ, and finally XQ. As with Tokina, Sigma used these abbreviations to alert buyers that these lenses represented higher quality items.

Sigma challenged patent restrictions imposed by Topcon, Leica and other camera makers and their success helped to create the active market for third-party lenses. However, none of their manual focus SLR lenses are cult classics and they are not highly collectible.

Soligor

Soligor was the trade mark for rebranded Japanese lenses distributed by the American Allied Impex Corporation after 1956. The company sourced lenses from several companies and users report that many Soligor lenses appear to have been manufactured by Tokina. Other users have noted lenses with similarities to those produced by Sigma, Sun and Makinon.

Soligor lenses were well regarded during the manual focus era, but are not highly collectible, but there is some interest in Soligor C/D lenses—an upgraded line developed to compete with Vivitar's Series 1 lenses—and TX mount lenses.

Coincidentally, Soligor should not be confused with the currently-active German company, Soligor GmbH, which adopted the name in 1993.

Spiratone

Spiratone was a Flushing, New York-based importer of rebranded Japanese photographic equipment. It prospered during the 1950s and 1960s, and many Spiratone branded items were sold through mail order. In addition, the company developed the Accura brand for wholesale distribution and owned the Sun brand in the United States.

Spiratone, Accura, and Sun lenses are not highly collectible, but interest has increased modestly since publication of *The History of Photography as Seen Through The Spira Collection* (New York: Aperture, 2001).

Star-D

Star-D was a house brand of Uniphot. Please see the company entry for additional details.

Sun

Sun Optical Company, Ltd., (Gotō Sun) was a Japanese lens manufacturer founded shortly after the Second World War. The company produced lenses in various mounts through the mid 1980s and ceased operation by the end of the decade. Sun lenses are not highly collectible and the company should not be confused with the currently active Korean firm of the same name.[5]

Super Carenar

Origins unknown.

Tamron

Tamron Company, Limited is a Japanese lens manufacturer founded as Taisei Optical Equipment Manufacturing in 1952 and renamed Tamron in 1959. In addition to producing lenses under its own name, Tamron also produced large numbers of lenses rebadged by distributors such as Accura, Vivitar, Spiratone and Cambron.

Historically, Tamron is best-known as developer of the T-Mount system which allows lenses to be used on any camera for which an adapter is available. Some commentators have suggested that the interchangeable lens mounts deserve cult status and consider them to be collectible.

In addition, a handful of Tamron lenses are considered to be highly collectible. Candidates include the 70-210 f2.8-4 manufactured in 1984,

---

5 One advance reader commented that "Sun Optical was the premier zoom lens manufacturer in the world. Most of the third-part Japanese zoom lenses sold under the various brand names in the 1960s were made by Sun."

the 90mm f2.5 macro lens, the 105mm f2.5 macro, the 300mm f5.6 with a close focus of only 5.5 feet, the 400mm f6.9 nesting lens,[6] and the 400mm f4 adaptall lens.

Technon

Technon is a trademark of Marukei Sangyo Company, Limited. Please see the company entry for additional details.

Teknon

Teknon is a trademark of Marukei Sangyo Company, Limited. Please see the company entry for additional details.

Tokina

Tokina is a Japanese optics company founded around 1955 by a group of Nikon engineers. If the oral history is correct, the story of Tokina's founding is nearly as interesting as that of Vivitar's flowering and has a happier ending.

At the time, there were few quality zooms available and conservative elements at Nikon planned to continue developing fixed focal length, prime lenses. A small group of dissident engineers wanted to develop high-quality zoom lenses and gave up the promise of life-time employment to found Tokina. Through the 1960s, Tokina produced lenses that were rebadged by other companies including Asanuma and Cambron as well as Vivitar. For Vivitar, the company produced the second version of the Series 1 70-210 f3.5 and Series 1 90mmf2.5 macro.

In the early 1970s, the company began to sell lenses with their own brand name and launched its Advanced Technology-Extra (AT-X) series of top quality lenses in 1981. Today, Tokina has a reputation for producing compact and rugged lenses. A handful of lenses are considered very desirable. Examples include the 90mm 2.5 AT-X macro lens that is optically identical to the original 90mm 2.5 Vivitar Series 1 macro lens, the "supersharp" 28-70mm f2.6-2.8 zoom designed by Angenieux, and the 28-85mm f4 RMC as well as the 28-85 f3.5-4.5 AT-X.

---

6 Nesting lenses collapse for storage. For example, the 400f6.9 collapsed from a full length of 16 inches to just 7 inches for storage in a camera bag.

Tou/Five Star

Tou/Five Star was a brand name used by Toyo Optics. Please see the company entry for additional information.

Tower

Tower was a brand name used by Sears for rebadged cameras, lenses and accessories. It appears that Ricoh was the primary manufacturer of Tower lenses for single lens reflex cameras.

There is considerable interest in Tower cameras, but Tower lenses for single lens reflex cameras are not highly collectible.

Toyo Optics

Toyo was an independent Japanese lens maker in the late 1960s and 1970s. Toyo Optics of the USA apparently was an American distributor and marketed lenses under three brand names: Toyo, Tou/Five Star and Toyo Five Star.

Toyo lenses are not highly collectible.

Uniphot

Uniphot was a Woodside, New York distributor of photographic equipment including lenses, cable releases, filters, tripods, and flash guns. The trademark was registered in 1973 and expired in 1994. Lenses appear to be rebranded generic pieces from Japan and are not highly collectible.

Zenitar

Zenitar lenses are produced by the Russian (formerly Soviet) firm JSC S. A. Zverev Krasnogorskiy Mekhanicheskiy Zavod founded in 1927. The firm currently produces a moderately well regarded 16mm lens, but its FD lenses are not highly collectible.

Zoomar and Zoomatar

Zoomar and Zoomatar are brand names associated with Kilfitt. Please see the company entry for additional details.

Zykkor

Zykkor is a trademark associated with the Pacemark Corporation. Please see the company entry for additional details.

Conclusion

Third-party lenses tell a fascinating part of the Canon story. The popularity of photography and the cost of Canon lenses spawned hosts of third-party manufacturers. Some made high quality optics and produced lenses that are cult classics. While several were unable to make the transition to autofocus lenses, a few made important contributions to the industry and knowledgeable collectors cherish their best lenses.

Other third-party manufacturers were mere imitators and cost cutters. Most have receded into well-deserved obscurity and informed collectors shun their lenses.

This chapter summarizes available information about many of the third-party manufacturers, but the full story has yet to be told. There were so many manufacturers and brand names that simply listing them all would be a ponderous task. There is a good chance you already have or will encounter lenses with names other than those mentioned here. When you do, please email me at ewskopec@yahoo.com and I will attempt to expand subsequent editions of this book.

Chapter 6: Managing Your Collection

It is easy to start collecting Canon manual focus SLRs, lenses, and accessories. Many people begin without even realizing that they have become collectors. They stumble across a camera in an antique store and buy it because it would look good on the desk. Others inherit a few odds and ends or receive a gift. One local collector got involved when he cleaned out a rental property and found a box of old cameras. I even know one collector who began by loaning a few dollars to a friend. A camera kit was collateral for the loan and became a collection when the friend didn't pay off the loan. Personally, I became a collector when a couple of used items caught my fancy while I was looking for modern equipment.

However you get started, what you include and how rapidly you build the collection is your decision alone. Collections can be large or small, tightly focused or widely varied, carefully planned or created "on the fly," all-consuming passions or free time avocations. As a result, there are few hard and fast rules. The only one to which I subscribe reflects the personal nature of collection—you should enjoy what you are doing!

Of course, there are lots of people around who will tell you what you should do. I'm not one of them! I have my own preferences and opinions, but I know you are far more interested in your own collection than mine.

That said, however, I know that there are some important decisions that you will have to make as you build your collection. The questions are the same ones every serious collector faces. I won't try to give you **the** answers, but I will try to help you understand the questions as well as the implications of your answers.

Pick Your Poison

It is easy to build quite a collection and even easier to keep adding to it. Once you get started, your collection may grow faster than you ever anticipated. Like bunnies in a hutch, the number seems to increase on its own. And like the bunnies, there may be neither rhyme nor reason in the accumulation.

Unless you have unlimited storage space, and money, you will eventually face the task of defining your collection. Again, there are neither right nor wrong answers and collectors have an incredible variety of choices. Some collect anything they find interesting. Others collect only specific camera models. I know one collector whose closets are full of plastic point and shoot cameras from the 1980s. Another has "only" six F-1s and every conceivable accessory. His closets are full too, but his two High Speed variants nestle in hermetically sealed display boxes.

The point is that you can define your collection however you want. Your own creativity is the best guide, but the practices of other experienced collectors may suggest some possibilities.

- I began by collecting Canon manual focus SLRs and have slowly branched out to include accessories and promotional materials plus a sampling of cult classic lenses.

- Another Canon enthusiast is fascinated by the progress of technology and collects only landmark cameras plus associated lenses and accessories.

- A friend collects only Kiron lenses and buys whatever bodies and accessories he needs to test them.

- An acquaintance aims to collect classic camera kits. In his collection, the late 50s are represented by a Canonflex RM with R mount lenses and a few accessories. The 60s feature an FP kit while the 70s are evidenced by a complete F-1 kit.

- Still another collector is enamoured by the EF. He has set out to collect all of the lenses and accessories mentioned in the EF user manual.

These examples are mentioned merely to suggest some definitions. Conversations with friends may suggest other possibilities and you may also enjoy visiting http://www.photographyhistory.com/idcclist.html, the International Directory of Camera Collectors. Look at how the collectors describe their interests and perhaps expand your review to other collector web sites.

However you define your collection, your decisions will affect what you buy and how you display the collection. If you define your collection loosely, you can probably find places for just about anything. On the other hand, if you define your collection narrowly, you probably will shop for a limited number of items and pass on things that don't fit.

My practice falls near the middle. I have a "wish list" of items I'm looking for, but also pick up other interesting pieces when I find them. My study walls are lined with framed print advertisements from the 60s and 70s, my desk sports a Canon ashtray, and a commemorative watch keeps time for me.

I'll say more about displaying your collection below. For the moment, please recognize that your definition will probably help to formalize your collection. Because my definition is relatively loose, I display the Canon bodies in chronological order with appropriate lenses and accessories nearby. The landmark camera collector displays cameras in order of technological innovation while the Kiron collector organizes his lenses by focal length and aperture. The kit collector has a separate shelf for each kit and the EF enthusiast has a pair of wall units that replicate images in the user manual.

Shelf Queens and Working Girls

Deciding whether or not to use the cameras, lenses, and accessories in your collection is another fundamental decision. Your choice will determine what you buy and how much repair or restoration you undertake.

There are the two sides of the coin. Pure collectors note that every time you take a piece off the shelf, you run the risk of damaging it or adding wear marks. This is important, they say, because pristine, unused cameras hold value far better than worn models. There are fewer new or mint items than used pieces, and the further one goes down the grading scale, the less a piece is worth.

Users/collectors agree, but note that "holding value" is not the only important consideration. For them, much of the pleasure in collecting comes from actually using the classics. And, they note, cameras and lenses deteriorate just sitting on the shelf. Shutters and apertures freeze from inactivity, foam deteriorates with age, and fungus attacks lens elements infrequently exposed to ultraviolet light.

For good or ill, things are not as simple as the two extremes suggest. There is lots of room on the edge of the coin and you may want to consider two additional factors.

First, some cameras have inherent limitations and are not necessarily fun to use. The Pellix and Pellix QL may be good examples. Even with fast lenses, their viewfinders are dim and their mirrors are fragile. I know a handful of users who disagree vehemently, but I concur with Peter Dechert who says that he has never met a happy user once the initial "glow" has faded.

Second, at today's prices, it makes sense to own both shelf queens and working girls. My collection includes a few mint, new-in-the-box items. Every other month or so, I take them off the shelf and run them through their tricks, but they never go in the field with me. For field use, I have functional but worn copies that are as much fun to use with much lower risk.

Code Blue: Bringing the Dead Back to Life

After you've decided what to include in your collection and whether or not you intend to use the pieces, it is helpful to think about your willingness to spend time and money repairing damaged items. The marketplace is full of cameras offered "as is," "for parts or repair," and "untested." These are all code words applied to cameras, lenses, and accessories that have stopped working for one reason or another. Many items have minor problems that the seller didn't want to address, but others have serious flaws. Some inoperative items may even be destined for second careers as paper weights and door stops.

With experience, you will learn to distinguish between the extremes and accurately appraise problems in between. At that point, you may make decisions on a case by case basis, but its still useful to think about the general question: is it worth your time and effort to bring a defective piece back to life?

Many collectors say No!, with great emphasis. They realize that its easy to confuse minor problems with serious defects and liken opening a damaged piece to sticking your hand into a barrel of snakes. Finding competent repair people is increasingly difficult, fragile parts are seldom available, and the cost of repairing a piece often exceeds its value. Equally important, many realize that they have neither the time nor the temperament to do the job themselves even if they have the tools, skills, and resources.

A smaller but equally enthusiastic group of collectors takes great pleasure in repairing damaged equipment. They note that inoperative cameras with even minor flaws sell for pennies on the dollar and they enjoy bringing classic pieces back to life. In addition to tools, spare parts, and manuals, many have developed substantial skills and a few even make a profit repairing cameras for other collectors or users.

In the final analysis, your own interests and temperament are the deciding factors. If you aren't sure, the easiest way to decide is by giving it a try. Damaged pieces are inexpensive, repair manuals and tools are readily available, and experienced collectors offer a wealth of advice. You may learn that you have a real knack for repairs. If not, you have learned a bit about yourself without spending a great deal of time or effort.

The Hunt is On!

Cameras, lenses, and accessories are where you find them. That may not sound like a particularly insightful statement, but it is an accurate description of the situation. In the 40 or 50 years since they left the factory, Canon manual focus SLRs have followed a variety of paths. Very few are in the hands of their first owners. They're advertised occasionally and one of the treasured kits in my collection is very close to a first owner set. It was originally sold to an American serviceman stationed in Japan. I know because the original Post Exchange receipt is still in the case. The original buyer used the kit sparingly and all of the pieces are in mint condition. Some are still wrapped in the original cellophane. The kit evidently spent a lot of time in the closet and was retrieved for an estate sale after the original owner passed away.

Cameras with such clear provenance are unusual. Most have passed through as many as 5 or 10 pairs of hands. Their original owners may have traded them in when they bought new equipment or passed them on to friends and relatives. Some found their way into the hands of students who traded them for video games and other ephemera. Today, many of these pieces turn up in antique or junk shops as well as garage sales.

The variety of journeys makes it difficult to know where cameras will "pop up." Nevertheless, there are a handful of places where you are most likely to find Canon manual focus SLRs, lenses, and accessories. Each venue has advantages and disadvantages and its up to you to decide how much time and effort you want to spend shopping at each. The list of places includes friends' and relatives' attics, garage and estate sales, antique shops, camera shows, newspaper and online classified advertisements, on-line auction sites, used equipment dealers, camera shops with selections of used equipment, and high end auctions like those at Christie's.

You may find interesting cameras at any of these spots. However, there is a trade-off between the time required to shop and the price you will pay. Dealers may have large inventories of carefully organized and graded equipment. Many repair and guarantee items and some will even search out rare or exotic pieces for you. Of course, you will pay a premium for these services and prices may be an order of magnitude higher than you would pay elsewhere.

Garage, rummage and estate sales as well as thrift stores are at the other end of the continuum. You can spend several days visiting local sales without finding a significant camera, lens, or accessory. When you do find them, there is a good chance they will be sitting in the bottom of a box with other clutter. After years of sitting in the former owner's closet, they are likely to be dirty and in need of service. Key pieces may be missing or scattered in several boxes. There is a good chance that old batteries have leaked leaving a layer of corrosion. There are no guarantees, but you can find real bargains and prices should be lower than at any other outlet.

Online and in person collectors groups occupy a middle point between the two extremes. Members refining or upgrading their collections regularly swap out items of lesser interest to them or dispose of whole collections when they decide to move on.

Personally, I enjoy attending camera shows and sorting through items at garage and estate sales. However, many of the items in my collection come from online auctions. eBay usually has a large selection of items and the search routine makes it relatively easy to find items of interest. Some tricks in buying on eBay are discussed below.

The Devil is in the Details

When you find an interesting piece, its up to you to determine what it is, what grade to assign, and whether or not it fits in your collection.

Well meaning but uninformed sellers seldom recognize distinctions that are important to collectors. Countless ads read "Canon film camera," "Canon camera with lens and flash," "antique Canon camera," "vintage Canon camera," and even "Canon camera with big lens." As engaging as these ads are, my all time favorite read "Canon New F-1n from 1971 with battery box and instructions."[1]

More knowledgeable sellers usually have more informative ads. However, even they miss distinctions between variants, fail to list lens apertures, and leave out accessory designations. Identifying the piece is up to you and it helps to be familiar with reliable sources like original product guides, users' manuals, Canon's online museum, and this book as well as a handful of other third party books.

After identifying a piece, your next task is to mentally assign a grade. You need not be as precise as resellers and merchants, but you should recognize cosmetic flaws, look for signs of rough handling and functional problems, and make sure you know what works and what doesn't. The Appendix offers more detailed suggestions for inspecting and grading Canon manual focus bodies, lenses, and accessories.

Finally, you should decide whether or not the piece deserves a place in your collection. The decision may be easy if you've defined your collection, determined whether you use collected items, established how much effort your are willing to invest in repair, and generated a list of items you are looking to add. However, don't let earlier decisions become straight jackets. Unique opportunities abound and undervalued items that don't fit your collection can become useful trading stock. Duplicate items can upgrade

---

1 On inspection, the camera turned out to be an original F-1 with a winder and part of the owner's guide for an EOS 630.

your collection. Sometimes its easier to buy a common body with interesting lens than to buy the lens alone. And, buying a "kit" is often the easiest way to add to your stock of accessories.

Only you can make these decisions and you can forgive yourself for occasional mistakes. After all, you aren't really "living on the edge." The modest danger of error is just part of the fun provided you learn from your mistakes.

Buying: Time is Money

While pondering these big questions, you may also want to think about your buying strategy. Again, there are two extremes while most collectors fall somewhere near the middle.

The fastest and easiest buying strategy is to pay whatever the seller asks. Akin to paying retail, this strategy requires little time and effort, and lets you get on with whatever else is on your agenda. The downside, of course, is that you may pay more than necessary and reduce the funds with which you could buy other items.

At the other extreme, some collectors never pay the asking price. They use all kinds of tactics to get better deals and ask for extras if the seller won't budge on price. They usually pay less than the rest of us, but at the cost of considerable time and effort.

Like most Canon collectors, my buying strategy falls somewhere between these extremes and varies from case to case. I'll pay the asking price if I think its reasonable and I'm in a rush. Sometimes, I even pay unreasonable prices for items that I really want. I'm also prepared to work hard when I want a particular piece. In one case, it took me nearly six weeks to buy one of the prized items in my collection—a pristine FP. The seller had it priced at nearly three times my target price and we spent a fair amount of time haggling. In the process we built a relationship and he eventually sold it to me because I "seemed like a pretty good guy." Other factors worked to my advantage; other potential buyers were put off by the asking price, he was convinced I'd provide a good home for a family heirloom, and I helped him sell a couple other items at nearly full price.

Underlying my strategy is a pretty good understanding of fair market value. I maintain a database of recent transactions and usually know what similar pieces are selling for. For example, in the last four months, 85 A-1s have been listed on eBay. The median selling price was $59 with high and low prices at $240 and $35. Comparing cameras with accessories to body-only sales complicates things a bit, but its easy to compensate if you know what the accessories alone sell for.

Figure 6.1 Recent A-1 Prices[2]

A-1	w 50f1.4 SSC	17	$83.82	02/28/11
A-1	w 50f1.4	13	$82.--	08/19/10
A-1	"outfit	7	$78.19	03/08/11
A-1	W 28&50 lens	16	$74.60	10/20/10
A-1	w 50f1.4	10	$73.--	10/06/10
A-1	W50f1.8 and flash	20	$72.--	11/15/10
A-1	w A2 winder	3	$71.--	11/24/10
A-1	BLACK serviced w warranty	7	$70.--	11/30/10
A-1	w 50f1.8 & flash	17	$69.77	07/28/10
A-1	w winder & "extras"	9	$66.99	08/06/10
A-1	w 50f1.8 & bellows	4	$66.--	04/01/11

Maintaining the database takes a modest amount of time, but I enjoy the activity and it does help me negotiate appropriate prices. And, I advise friends who reciprocate by helping me with other concerns.

Selecting a buying strategy, determining how to apply it, and deciding how much work to do are all decisions that you alone can make. My approach works for me, but you may have different needs and preferences. Whatever you decide, its easy to refine your strategy as you gain experience.

To eBay or not to eBay . . .

that is the question.

I'm sure Shakespeare would forgive me for stealing his elegant prose if he knew how important the question is to collectors. In recent years, eBay has emerged as the world's largest marketplace for Canon manual focus SLRs, lenses, and accessories. Every day, roughly 50 potentially collectible

2 The second column lists bundled items while the final three columns are the number of bidders, sales price, and date the auction closed.

pieces change hands and about as many are added to the sales roster. It is easy to use eBay search routines and users can follow nearly a thousand transactions at a time without even bidding.

For all its virtues, eBay has some detractors. They're easy to spot in online forums because they refer to the site as "fleaBay." I'm not a member of the group, but understand their worries. The decision to buy on eBay is up to you and I suspect your decision will depend on your reactions to five concerns.

First, buying on eBay requires you to have considerable faith in faceless sellers. Most are reputable and well intentioned, but there is a very small number of less scrupulous sellers. Risk arises from sending money to people you've never met on the basis of their descriptions, promises, and photographs. eBay has done a great deal to moderate the risks: buyer feedback, dispute resolution, and the PayPal system. But all of those measures take time and you may not be satisfied with the outcomes. Personally, I never buy anything worth more than $50 from a seller I don't know. The limit goes up as I learn to trust regular sellers.

Second, eBay is not a pure auction and some buyers have learned to "game" the system. They use an approach known as "sniping." They follow items in a "Watch" list but don't bid until the last few seconds. They bid just as auctions close and hope to "steal" items before other bidders can respond.

This can be very frustrating for the uninitiated who approach bidding as they would in other auctions. They bid early and often, topping opposing bidders whenever someone else enters the auction. After several days without competitive bids, they assume they have won. Most are surprised by a wave of competitive bids just as the auction closes.[3]

Third, you need to learn to live with reserve prices. Even if an auction runs its course, sellers are not obligated to sell an item unless the final bid

---

3 There are now several software packages that automate the sniping process. As a result, prices jump dramatically in the final few seconds of auctions as software agents compete with one another. In some auctions, as much as 85% of the final price is realized in the final few seconds. Coincidentally, setting your bid limit high enough that agents can't easily jump it is the only defensive measure I've found.

exceeds an unpublicized minimum. My guess is that about 30% of Canon manual focus SLRs, lenses, and accessories end without a sale because the final bid is lower than the reserve price. This irritates buyers who would have paid more and don't fully understand the system.[4]

Fourth, a significant number of Canon manual focus SLRs, lenses, and accessories are listed with "Buy-It-Now" prices and "Make-An-Offer" options. In general, Buy-It-Now prices are higher than the seller hopes to realize through the auction process and some may not even consider reasonable offers. Personally, I evaluate Buy-It-Now prices in terms of fair market prices and use make-an-offer options sparingly.

Finally, it helps to realize that eBay prices are cyclical. Prices for Canon manual focus bodies, lenses, and accessories are generally high during the last two weeks of November and first week of December. It appears that people are looking for Christmas gifts and use other venues once it will be difficult to assure an item will arrive in time. There is also a monthly cycle with higher prices early in the month before buyers' budgets get stressed and lower near the end of the month. In addition, prices of relatively rare pieces fluctuate with the interests of active collectors. Call it a "flavor of the month" phenomenon. EFs were in high demand for a while followed by F-1s and prices are now appreciating for earlier models like the FX, FP, and Pellix.

Ultimately, your comfort buying on eBay depends on your ability to recognize and cope with these phenomena. You may also want to consider the availability of Canon manual focus gear through other channels. I live in an area were few are available and prices are excessive. As a result, I make extensive use of eBay, but your situation may be different.

Cosmetic Surgery

Another important question concerns cosmetic restoration. Again the extremes are easy to describe, but not particularly informative. At one extreme, a few collectors maintain their Canon manual focus SLRs just as they were found. Personally, I don't find dust and grime to be particularly

---

4 Occasionally an email to the seller can open direct negotiations, but many items are re-listed and you may find them in subsequent auctions.

attractive, but I'm even less enamoured by the other extreme. A few—very few—collectors aim to restore their cameras to factory new cosmetic condition. They disassemble the cameras, replace dinged or scratched parts or sand and repaint/rechrome exposed surfaces, replace the coverings. Unethical ones may even try to pass off their products as mint or new items.

Most collectors stick to the middle of the road. Personally, I clean exposed surfaces and regularly re-cement loose coverings. Occasionally, I replace broken or damaged parts, but I stop short of repainting and replating.[5]

The best memory …

is not as good as the palest ink, or so the Chinese proverb reminds us. Nevertheless, a few collectors hold details of their collection in memory. Point to any item in their collection and they can tell you when and where they bought it, how much they paid, and why they added it to their collection.

Few collectors have such facile memories and most have some sort of record keeping system. Some keep boxes of receipts or note cards. Others record their purchases in spiral bound notebooks or use word processing or spreadsheet programs. A growing number use databases.

Unless you are one of the lucky few with prodigious memories, you will probably feel most comfortable with some sort of record keeping system. Deciding which to use is up to you, but each has advantages and disadvantages:

- Boxes of receipts are the simplest system to create and maintain. Just drop the paper in the box every time you add to your collection. Sadly, finding individual receipts a month or more later can consume all the energy you saved in the first place.

- Spiral bound notebooks can be used as a journal listing additions to your collection in chronological order. It takes a little more effort than dropping materials in a box, but it is usually much easier to find individual records.

---

5 The Appendix has some suggestions for cleaning Canon manual focus gear.

- Note cards are a modest improvement on chronological journals. They can be arranged to suit your current needs and can even be kept with the items to provide captions. Sadly, notecards are easy to lose and you may not even realize that one or two are missing until you need them.

- Spreadsheet and document files are a greater improvement on re-cord books. Add items to them as you would to a journal and then sort them to suit your purposes. You can even carry a printout with you while shopping. Spreadsheets are more flexible than docu-ments, but search routines in both make it easy to find individual items.

- Finally, if you are comfortable with the software, databases are the most comprehensive and flexible record keeping system. Once you have configured the database, you merely add a record every time you add an item to your collection. You can find individual records very quickly, print a variety of reports, and even print out labels for the pieces in your collection.[6]

Figure 6.2 Sample Database Record

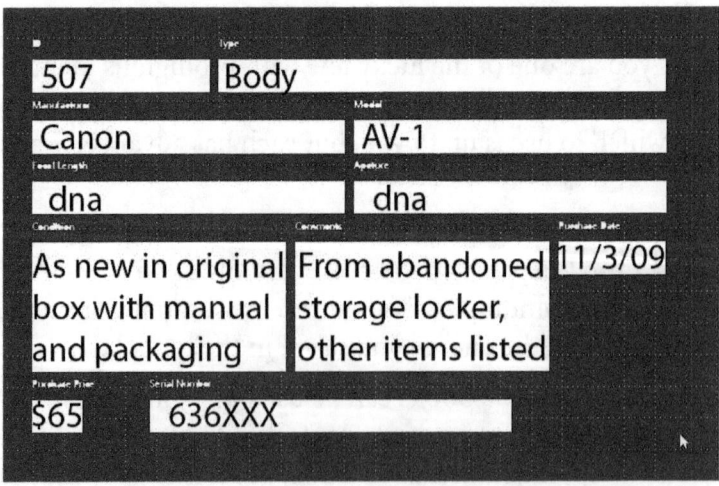

_____

6 Check http://www.downloads.com for pre-configured databases for collectibles and remember to back up your database to avoid losing everything when your computer crashes.

I've used all five systems and now record everything in a database. I like the flexibility, but ultimately the choice is yours. If you aren't sure what will work best for you, try each and settle on the system you prefer.

Treat your cameras like friends …

display each in its best light.

Where and how you display your collection is the last decision we'll mention here. Like the others, your answer is personal, but the practices of other collectors may suggest some possibilities.

Collectors have an enormous variety of approaches. Some keep their Canon collectibles in storage boxes and bring them out only for specific purposes. Others display everything they have in enclosed cases, on open shelves, and in small lucite display cases. Some exhibit their collections on desk tops, room dividers, and book shelves. Others have crafted shadow boxes and hang pieces in place of photos or paintings.

Figure 6.3 A Shadowbox Display

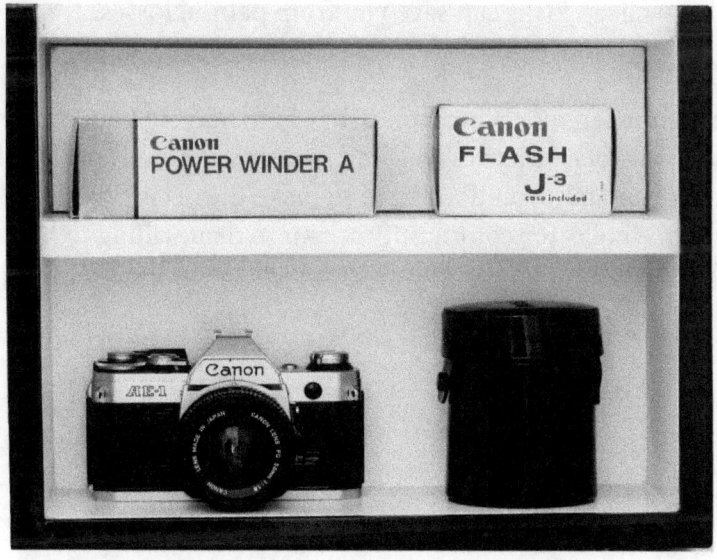

Most accomplished collectors mix these practices. They display prime pieces in appropriate cases, leave less valuable pieces in the open, and store users and defective pieces out of sight. The possibilities are limited only by your creativity. However, you should choose alternatives that protect your Canon manual focus SLRs from their principal enemies:

- Moisture; if you live in an area with high humidity, your collection should reside in a sealed and dehumidified enclosures.

- Dust; protect your collection from air borne dust with glass or plastic enclosures.

- Fungus; do not store clean lenses with infected ones

- Heat; keep your collection out of direct sunlight in a relatively cool area.

- Accidental drops; store items where they won't accidently get knocked off the shelf when you are working nearby.

- Fingerprints; if your collection is handled regularly, keep a clean, dry rag handy.

Depending on where you display your collection, security may also be an issue. Even cheap locks can save you from painful losses.

Conclusion

These are the ten most common issues in managing your collection. I'm sure you will face others as well and mastering them is part of the joy of collecting. Fortunately, you don't have to make the decisions alone. Active members of the collector community are more than willing to help and you can contact them through the online forums listed in the Bibliography.

Appendix

Inspecting, grading, and cleaning are all important considerations. Inspection alerts you to potential flaws in Canon manual focus gear and helps you avoid buying damaged equipment. Understanding grades makes it easier to determine fair market prices, value your collection, and conduct transactions with other buyers and sellers. Finally, appropriate cleaning makes your equipment more serviceable and may even convert dingy relics into dazzling collectibles.

Space was unfortunately limited at earlier spots so this Appendix has somewhat longer discussions of each. The expositions are as complete as space allows and cover the basics in a way that will let you learn more on your own.

Inspecting

In general, Canon manual focus bodies, lenses, and accessories were designed for long service lives and made to stand up to heavy use. Many are functioning perfectly after forty or more years of use. The most fortunate pieces have belonged to conscientious photographers who used them with care, serviced them regularly, and stored them in clean, sheltered environments.

Other items have been less fortunate. Careless users have dropped them, carried them in bags without dividers, stored them with little protection from dust or moisture, ignored service requirements, attempted repairs with little knowledge and less skill, and simply tossed them aside when they stopped working properly.

Today, most Canon manual focus bodies, lenses, and accessories come to market without any information about prior owners. As a result, you seldom know how many people owned the equipment, how frequently they used it, or how well they cared for it. Moreover, the uncertainty is likely to be greatest at the least expensive venues: garage sales, flea markets, and online auctions.

Fortunately, you don't need a detective to ferret out key points in the equipments' life stories. All Canon manual focus bodies, lenses, and accessories carry important clues with them. If you know what to look for, you can identify signs of good or ill treatment and avoid the worst potential dangers. Most experienced collectors have inspection routines that help them spot flaws that may not be apparent on first glance. Their routines include three simple tests for all equipment along with more detailed checks for bodies and lenses.[1]

Figure A.3 General Equipment Checklist

Shake Test	Mentioned in Chapter 6, a gentle shake is a good way to check for loose or missing pieces as well as unseen damage. Put your fingers on things that should be loose–like the film rewind lever–shake gently, and listen carefully. Rattles suggest loose or broken parts as well as unskilled repairs. Personally, I consider equipment with unexplained rattles to be suitable only for parts.
Sniff Test	Unusual smells are good indicators of improper storage or repairs. Mold, mildew and smoke suggest improper storage while solvent, cleaner and paint smells may be remnants of excessive cleaning, hidden repairs, or repainting. Improper lubricants also leave tell tale scents. Many amateur restorers use WD-40 which leaves residue on sensitive parts and some collectors have even found vegetable cooking oil used in place of appropriate lubricants.
Consistency Test	As prices climb, inventive restorers occasionally mix parts from different models. Their products may be serviceable–at least for a while–but experienced collectors will spot the inconsistencies quickly. To protect yourself, carry a copy of the users' guide with you and make sure all of the components are consistent with original specifications.

Most Canon bodies are pretty sturdy, but some have been damaged over the years. Cameras with misaligned components, broken pieces, and un-noted repairs come to the market frequently. Reputable sellers advertise them as "parts" cameras and grade them appropriately. Unfortunately,

---

1 The following checklists are based on my own experiences and readings as well as those of other knowledgeable collectors. Members of the Yahoo Group, camera-fix, added a number of points and I appreciate their contributions.

some flaws escape notice and less honorable sellers may try to disguise the problems.

To guard against getting "burned," many experienced collectors begin by examining the camera's general appearance and proceed to look at internal features, shutter performance, and other functions.

Figure A.4 Body Checklist

External Appearance

Always remove the ever ready case and then check the following:

- Dents, dings, scrapes and scratches suggest that previous owners have been careless and greater problems may surface.

- Names and numbers engraved, etched or scratched onto a body reduce cosmetic appeal and perceived value.

- Brassing is a common sign of heavy use and you will frequently see it on bodies used by professionals. It is not necessarily a problem if the camera has been serviced regularly, but it does reduce cosmetic appeal and perceived value.

- Loose, torn, or obviously re-cemented body coverings are signs of careless use, improper storage and undocumented repairs.

- Missing screws and open holes indicate that pieces are missing or an unskilled person has tinkered with the body.

- Gaps between parts and other alignment problems are signs of inexpert repairs and part substitutions.

- Discolored metal components are indicators of excessive cleaning and improper storage.

- Dust and haze in the viewfinder complicate focusing, but may be acceptable. However, cracks and out of place meter components indicate that the camera has been ill treated and other problems are likely to surface.

Internal Features

Avoid touching either the shutter or mirror, and:

- Open the battery compartment (if there is one) and check for corrosion and damaged electrical contacts that suggest batteries have leaked. Simple cleaning may suffice but pitted components herald expensive repairs.

- Shutter curtains should be smooth without wrinkles, patches or holes. Metal shutter slats should be straight and clean. Pass on cameras with off track shutters hanging at weird angles.

- Film rails should be clean and smooth. Pits and/or gummy accumulations point to improper storage and herald expensive repairs.

- Film pressure plates should be smooth and clean, and spring back into place when depressed.

- Film take up sprockets should move smoothly and easily when film is advanced. Chipped pins suggest excessive pressure has been applied and broken tips may have fallen into other parts of camera.

- Light seals and mirror bumpers should be soft and flexible. Those that have dried can be replaced easily but tacky ones may have spread goo throughout the camera. This can require disassembling for a thorough cleaning or other expensive repairs.

Shutters

The shutter is the most sensitive component of a body and even minor problems can lead to costly repairs. You don't need specialized equipment to recognize the most common problems.

- Before you close the film door, set the shutter speed to B and press the shutter button. The shutter curtain should stay open and the mirror move up out of the optical path (except with the Pellix and Pellix QL).

- Remove the lens and set the shutter to its highest speed. Look through the shutter while you press the shutter button. Brightness at either end indicates that the shutter curtains aren't traveling at the same speed and expensive repairs will be required.

Then close the film door and listen carefully while activating the shutter.

- At its fastest speed, you should hear a crisp, audible snap.

- Test fire at different speeds and you should hear an audible difference. Slower speeds will be progressively less crisp and you may even test the slowest speeds with your watch.

- You may also hear the "Canon squeak" as the mirror moves up. Its not a major problem but suggests lubrication is needed.

Other Functions

Other functions vary with bodies and its a good idea to review users' guides so you know which should be available. Be sure to check the following:

- Film advance should be smooth and even.

- All dials should move freely. Stiffness or binding point to dried lubricants and the need for costly repairs.

- Meters should respond to changes in aperture, shutter speed, and film speed. Readings should be consistent with the lighting conditions and you may check them against a hand-held meter.

- Film counter wheels should return to zero when the back is opened.

- Self-timers should operate smoothly and you can check the delay against your watch.

- Test the multiple exposure button.

- Check the depth of field preview.

- Make sure the mirror-up function works.

- Mount a lens you know is good and check both infinity and close focus.

- Install a flash and make sure it fires properly.

Lenses have fewer moving parts and damage is more likely to be evident. Nevertheless, systematic inspection will save you heartache and needless expense.

As we noted in Chapter 3, the designations on Canon lenses tell you a good deal about them. Begin by reviewing the data to make sure the lens is a model you want to add to your collection. Remember, Canon produced several iterations of popular lenses as well as consumer grade lenses with smaller maximum apertures than higher quality lenses of the same focal length. Then examine the external surface as well as mechanical and optical elements.

Figure A.5 Lens Check List

External Appearance

- Lettering should be clear and legible; modest paint wear is normal, but avoid lenses with significant scrapes or dings.

- Repainting may be acceptable, but is often evidence of extensive repairs.

- The lens mount should be consistent with published descriptions. Bent levers and missing pins are evidence of careless handling and unskilled repairs.

- Dents, dings, and abrasions around the filter ring are common and may not interfere with lens operation. However, they suggest careless handling and more serious problems may surface later.

Mechanical Elements

- Zooms should move freely without binding, but still be firm enough to avoid slipping in use.

- Focus rings should turn easily without catching or binding. Stiff rings result from impact damage or dried lubricants. In either case, disassembly may be required.

- Aperture stops should click into place with modest resistance to turning through the entire range of stops.

- Aperture blades should be dry with no sign of oil.

- Aperture blades should open and close uniformly and move freely as you change apertures.

- If possible, mount lenses on a body and make sure they will focus to infinity and the aperture blades open and close when shooting.

Optical Elements

Begin by examining the front element at an oblique angle so the light "dances" across the surface. Look for the following:

- Chips and deep scratches seriously degrade images and reduce perceived lens value substantially.

- Cleaning marks are generally concentric lines on the lens surface caused by improper cleaning. Modest marks will have minimal effect on images but heavy marks reduce perceived value substantially.

- Avoid lenses with discolored patches on element surfaces. Lens coatings have been damaged and elements may need to be replaced.

- Repeat the same checks on the rear lens element.

Then, shine a strong light through the lens and look for the following:

- Dust flecks are common in older lenses. Modest amounts are acceptable, but densities large enough to affect optical performance reduce perceived value.

- Spots with spreading tendrils on elements within the lens are fungus. Modest amounts may be cleaned after disassembling the lens, but fungus can etch element surfaces and may require replacement.

- Avoid lenses with discolored areas near the edges of elements. Elements have begun to separate and replacing them is costly and time consuming if you can even find replacement parts.

- Avoid lenses that appear foggy. Whatever its cause, it is likely to get worse without substantial and expensive repairs.

Collectors show more interest in Canon manual focus bodies and lenses than in most accessories. Yet accessories should be tested as well and unique tests apply to each. For example, flashes should power up quickly with fresh batteries and "pop" cleanly when fired, accessory meters should respond predictably to changes in light, and bellows should be flexible and free of pinholes. Original users' guides are the best source of information about accessories and you should make sure that each does what it is supposed to do.

Having said all of that rather quickly, four caveats are worth noting. First, no one can guarantee equipment that passes these tests will function well in the future. Fragile parts and electrical components may be on their last legs and fail after testing. In addition, some pieces may malfunction in particular situations and the variations are too numerous to test in advance.

Second, identifying minor flaws doesn't necessarily mean you should pass on a piece. Items with cosmetic flaws may work perfectly and noting the imperfections can help you negotiate better deals.

Third, with appropriate skills, you may be able to repair many of the items I've suggested you avoid. Repairing defective equipment for yourself and others can be an enjoyable and profitable hobby. Before you decide, take a look at resources available at http://tech.groups.yahoo.com/group/camera-fix/ and elsewhere.

Finally, rare items may be collectible even with major defects. You may hope to repair them some day, but for the time being they can be historically significant reminders of earlier practices.

Grading

As noted in the Introduction, camera grading is somewhat subjective. Remember, condition is in the eye of the beholder. Even experienced collectors disagree with one another from time to time, and the same rater may assign different grades to the same piece on different days.[2]

Nevertheless, commonly accepted rating schemes are important touchstones for collectors and users alike. As more equipment is sold online, grading scales help to establish common expectations, suggest reasonable sales prices, and should alert buyers to noteworthy faults.

---

2 Rater reliability is problematic in many areas that depend on human judgment. Researchers in the social sciences have struggled with it for some time and an Internet search on "rater reliability" will produce numerous articles.

There are two common rating scales. The first is a verbal system developed by *Shutterbug Magazine.* It is easy to understand and popular with both merchants and collectors.

The *Shutterbug* scheme recognizes eight grades from New and Mint at the top to Ugly at the bottom. Figure A.1 lists the grades from best to worst.

Figure A.1 *Shutterbug* Magazine's Rating Scheme

New	Never sold to a customer and never used. New as shipped by the manufacturer or distributor with all original packing and instruction manuals. Merchandise sold as "NEW" must be eligible for full warranty service from the authorized importer/distributor in the USA.
MINT	100% original finish. Just like factory new, but may not include original packing material or instruction books.
EX+	90-99% of original finish. Used very little, but obviously used. No major marring of the finish or brassing. Optics perfect. Mechanics perfect.
EX	80-89% of original finish. May have a finish flaw or two which detract from appearance, but must be optically and mechanically perfect.
EX-	70-79% of original finish. May have relatively large flaws in finish which do not affect function. Must be optically and mechanically perfect.
GOOD	60-69% of original finish. Must be complete, but may be scratched or scuffed. Metal may show wear but should have no corrosion, rust or pits. Must be optically and mechanically perfect.
FAIR	50-59% of original finish. May or may not be perfectly functional, but all functional defects must be clearly stated in the ad. Would not be attractive to the eye.
UGLY	50% or less original finish. Well used and worn. May have missing parts or may not be fully functional.

The *Shutterbug* scheme is probably the most widely used rating system, but some people prefer numerical grades. I find them somewhat more difficult to apply, but their proponents argue they permit finer distinctions. Figure A.2 displays a representative numerical scheme.

Figure A.2 Numerical Ratings

10	Brand new, unused with all original packing, paperwork, and, accessories.
9+	New and unused, but missing warranty cards, instructions, or minor accessories.
9	Used, but "like-new" and well cared for. Optics and mechanics are perfect, but original packaging, paperwork, or minor accessories are missing.
9-	Lightly used with one or two minor cosmetic flaws.
8+	Used gear in above average condition. It may have minor cosmetic flaws but is very clean while the optical and mechanical elements are perfect.
8	Mechanically and optically perfect, but used on a regular basis with noticable wear and evident cosmetic flaws. Many collectors consider this to be "average" and equate it to EX in the *Shutterbug* scheme.
8-	Mechanically and optically perfect equipment that shows higher than average usage. Brassing, scratches, and other cosmetic flaws are pronounced.
7+	User grade equipment showing signs of heavy usage including brassing and scratches. Lenses may show wipe marks that do not substantially degrade image quality. Mechanical functions all work, but squeaks may be noticable, especially on A Series bodies.
7	Cosmetically, the equipment shows signs of heavy usage—significant brassing, scratches, and maybe a few minor dents. Optically, there will be some scratches on the glass which may affect picture quality (but not too badly). Mechanically, the equipment must be in complete working order.

<7	Equipment below 7 is unlikely to be collectible unless there are extenuating circumstances. Commonly described as "battered" or "ugly," lower grade pieces typically have noticable mechanical and/or optical problems along with dents and severe cosmetic flaws. Collectors may buy these items as "parts" cameras but few display pieces at these grades unless they are exceedingly rare.

Both verbal and numeric rating scales aim to make ratings less subjective and provide common points of reference. Those are laudable objectives, but collectors should realize that neither scale is magic. Grading depends on the skill and integrity of the rater, and no scheme can eliminate human frailties.

A couple caveats are worth noting as well.

Some merchants add further refinements. For example, Keh.com adds DEMO "As packaged by manufacturer complete with manufacturer's USA warranty. Never owned by a consumer but used for demonstration." Other sellers add AI or "as is" for damaged or defective equipment sold without warranties. A modest group of merchants use "else" to note particular defects. For example, an EF in my collection has a damaged pentaprism and the seller accurately described it as "dented pentaprism else EX+."

You may also see items described as "reconditioned" or "refurbished." Neither term is defined precisely and you should always determine what the rater means. A few sellers confuse cleaning with reconditioning while others include lubrication and adjustment as well as testing. While you are checking, it is also wise to find out who worked on the equipment and what warranties they provide.

While both verbal and numerical systems are commonplace, a few sellers invent their own or use strings of undefined adjectives. "Very clean," "exceptional," "superb," "outstanding," "beautiful," and "nice" often color their descriptions. Sellers who don't specialize in cameras may be unaware of the common ratings, but others choose not to use them. I am always wary of "off the cuff" rating systems because they are seldom well defined and defeat the purpose of grading. As a result, I seldom buy from sellers who depart substantially from accepted practice.

Cleaning

Almost every Canon manual focus body, lens, and accessory will benefit from a thorough cleaning. Dull metal surfaces, smudged viewfinders, dry or faded coverings, accumulated grime in grooves and serrations, and prominent fingerprints all contribute to a decrepit look. Even exceptional pieces may lack "sparkle" and run of the mill items may look like junk.

How much cleaning you do is up to you. As we noted in Chapter 6, a few collectors maintain their Canon manual focus equipment in "as found" condition while a handful of others aim for complete restoration. Most collectors have adopted an intermediate standard. They aim to clean to the original surface without damaging it. The qualification—without damaging the original surface—is extremely important. Valuable and historically important pieces can be irreparably damaged by excessive cleaning with inappropriate materials.

Doing it right can and should be a time consuming process. Nevertheless, the rewards are considerable and the least attractive pieces often benefit most from a thorough job. My own approach has evolved over the years and yours probably will as well. The following suggestions begin with a list of things you should never do followed by a list of recommended supplies and conclude with a simple procedure that avoids most common pitfalls.

Never DOs

- Never use abrasive cleansers or harsh solvents. They may make the process faster, but there is too much danger of damaging the underlying surface.

- Never use abrasive scrubbing pads, steel wool, metal brushes, or emery paper. Again, there is too much danger of damaging the underlying surface.

- Never spray any liquids including solvents or lubricants directly on a piece; fluids easily seep inside where they gum up mechanical components or damage electrical connections. Instead, spray solvents onto a cloth or cotton swab and apply lubricants with the end of a tooth pick or a small hypodermic needle.

- Never open the film door or remove a lens before you brush off exterior surfaces. Particles of surface grime can fall into the inner workings and cause problems.

- Never use canned air or air compressors to blow out the inside of a piece. Sprays of canned air may leave a residue and high pressure bursts can damage or dislodge parts. Instead, use a squeeze bulb so you can control the pressure.

- Never touch the shutter curtains. They are among the most fragile components of a camera and can be damaged easily.

- Never touch the mirror or anything in the mirror box. Again, they are easily damaged and oil from your fingers can degrade mirror surfaces. If you absolutely must clean the mirror, try using a small amount of soapy water on a cotton swab and rub gently.

- Never force anything. It is too easy to break fragile parts. Unless you are confident of your abilities, jammed components are best dislodged by qualified repair people.

- Never disassemble anything if you are not sure you can get it back together. Just to be on the safe side, take photos as you work so you have a piece by piece guide for reassembly.

- Never use unsuitable tools. They can damage parts and leave marks on exposed surfaces.[3]

Cleaning Materials

Most of the appropriate cleaning materials are readily available in drug and hardware stores. They are so common that you probably have most of them around the house already. Here are the things most experienced collectors use.

---

3 Be especially careful in selecting screw drivers. JIS (Japanese Industry Standard) screw heads look like more familiar Philips head screws, but the two do not mate correctly.

- A shallow pan or tray at least 12 by 18 inches.

- A small squeeze blower.

- Artists or cosmetic brushes in various sizes.

- A good supply of clean, lint free rags.

- A couple **soft** toothbrushes.

- A supply of cotton swabs.

- A few toothpicks.

- One or two pencils with fresh erasers.

- Windex® and/or isopropyl alcohol.

- Well diluted liquid dish soap.

- A roll of narrow masking tape.

- Leather dressing.

- Liquid black shoe polish.

- Lens cleaner.

- Lens tissue.

- A bottle of rubber cement.

Process

I have a small work table set aside for cleaning cameras, but any stable surface in a clean, well lighted area will work. Be sure to redirect fans as well as heating and air conditioning vents away from your work area. I always work in a low metal pan with a clean rag on the bottom. The pan keeps pieces from rolling off the table and the rag prevents scarring. Once set up, the process unfolds as follows:

1. Quickly remove loose surface particles with the squeeze blower and soft brushes.

2. Using a rag moistened with Windex®, wipe down the exterior surface.

3. Remove resistant grime with a toothbrush moistened with Windex. Knurled surfaces on dial edges and lens rings often have accumula-

tions and its may require several applications of solvent. Quickly dry the surface between applications to keep fluids from migrating into the body, lens, or accessory.

4. Open the film door and remove the lens, then gently blow out the interior. Be sure to rotate the body and direct air at the base or the take up sprocket to remove film chips.

5. Using a rag moistened with isopropyl alcohol, gently wipe the rails and film plate. Be careful not to touch the shutter curtains or anything in the mirror box. Remember, its better to repeat the process several times with damp rags than to let excess fluid run into the piece.

6. Remove dust and lint from foam seals and the mirror bumper with masking tape. Press gently and repeat the process as necessary.

7. Gently clean electrical contacts with pencil erasers. Remember to hold the piece so dust and shavings fall outside.

8. If necessary, remove grime under loose edges of the body covering and re-cement them with rubber cement.

9. If necessary, touch up the body covering with liquid black shoe polish. Use only moderate amounts, wipe it off and let the covering dry overnight.

10. Make sure the body cap, film door, and battery cover are sealed tightly and apply leather dressing to the body covering. Use small amounts and rub gently. Remember, it is better to apply several light coatings than one heavy coating.

11. Let the piece sit over night and wipe it down with a clean rag before putting it in your display cabinet or storage area.

The specific steps and the amount of time spent on each varies from piece to piece. Your common sense is as good a guide as any.

Conclusion

Repairs are beyond the scope of this book and I know there are others that are more skilled than I. Fortunately, there are several good books on the subject and copies of Canon's original repair directions are now available from several sources. In addition, a number of websites have directions for specific repairs and I've listed several of them in the Bibliography.

As I've said before, repairing Canon manual focus bodies, lenses, and accessories can be an enjoyable and rewarding hobby. If you decide to give it a try, buy a couple AS IS pieces and polish your skills before you tackle more expensive projects.

Bibliography

The following pages list many of the sources on which I've relied. I've listed the books that have stuck with me, even those about cameras by other manufacturers. In addition to being valuable sources of information, many are enjoyable reading and deserve prominent places on your bookshelves.

Canon's instructions and product brochures are among the most informative sources. All are more reliable than the brief descriptions posted on Canon's Virtual Museum (http://www.canon.com/camera-museum/camera/index.html) and building your own set is a worthwhile pastime.

Internet users' groups and forums distill the experiences and insights of knowledgeable collectors and users. Members of the FD Forum fact checked this manuscript and I barely scratched the surface of the group's accumulated wisdom. In addition, many groups have archives of useful information as well as sets of interesting links.

Finally, I've listed a handful of informative web sites.

Books

Anon. *The Canon Camera Handbook*. Somerville, Mass.: Curtin & London, Inc., 1981.

Baczynsky, Mark. *How to Restore Antique and Classic Cameras, with Tips on Collecting, Trading, and Selling.* Kingston, N.Y. : Embee Press, 1977.

Ball, David. *The New F-1 World*. Canon, 1982.

Cecchi, Danilo. *Asahi Pentax and Pentax SLR 35mm Cameras: 1952-1989* Hove, Sussex: Hove Foto Books, 1990.

Canon. *Lenswork*. Canon, 1986.

Crawley, Geoffrey. *Canon F-1 System And Accessories*. Garden City, N.Y., Amphoto, 1973.

Dechert, Peter. *Canon Single Lens Reflex Cameras 1959-1991*. Yakima, Washington: Historical Camera Publications, 1992.

Dechert, Peter. *Canon Rangefinder Cameras 1933-68*. Hove, East Sussex, U.K. : Hove Foto Books, 1985.

Emanuel, W. D. *Canon Reflex Guide*. London: The Focal Press, 1970.

Francke, Harald. *Complete Canon User's Guide; Modern Classics*. Guernsey, Channel Islands: Hove Photo Books ltd., 1996.

Faragher, Scott. *Cameras for Collectors*. Atglen, PA: Schiffer Publishing, 2002.

Gustavson, Todd. *Camera: A History of Photography from Daguerreotype to Digital*. New York : Sterling Innovation, 2009.

Jonas, Paul. T*he Canon, Canonet, Canonflex Manual*. New York, Universal Photo Books, 1961.

Jonas, Paul. *The Canon Manual*. Garden City, N.Y., Amphoto, 1973.

Jonas, Paul. *The Canon Manual*; Rev. ed. Garden City, N.Y. : Amphoto, 1976.

Laurance, Mike. *The Canon Guide*. New York, N.Y. : Amphoto, 1979.

Levy, Michael. *Selecting and Using Classic Cameras: A User's Guide to Evaluating Features, Condition & Usability of Classic Cameras*. Buffalo, N.Y.: Amherst Media, Inc., 2002.

Lippincott, Joe. *Care and Repair of Classic Cameras for Photographers and Collectors*. Quincy, MA : J. Lippincott, 1999.

Long, Brian. *Nikon: A Celebration*. Ramsbury, Marlborough, Wittshire, U.K.: The Crowood Press, Ltd., 2006.

Long, Brian. *Canon: A Celebration*. Ramsbury, Marlborough, Wittshire, U.K.: The Crowood Press, Ltd., 2008.

Matanle, Ivor. *Collecting and Using Classic Cameras*. New York : Thames and Hudson, 1996.

McBroom, Michael. *McBroom's Camera Bluebook, 6th ed*. Buffalo, N.Y. Amherst Media, 2000.

McKeown, James M., and Joan C. McKeown, eds. *McKeown's Price Guide to Antique and Classic Cameras, 2005-2006*.

Pasi, Alessandro. *Leica: Witness to a Century*. New York : W.W. Norton, 2004.

Shell, Bob. *Canon Compendium*. East Sussex: Hove Books, 1994.

Shell, Bob, and Harold Francke. *Canon Classic Cameras*. Rochester, New York: Magic Lantern, 1994.

Shipman, Carl. *How to Select & Use Canon SLR Cameras*. Tucson, Arizona: Fisher Publishing, Inc., 1979.

Tomosy, Thomas. *Camera Maintenance & Repair, Book 1: Fundamental Techniques: A Comprehensive, Fully Illustrated Guide*. Buffalo, N.Y.: Amherst Media, Inc., 1999.

Tomosy, Thomas. *Camera Maintenance & Repair, Book 2: Advanced Techniques: A Comprehensive, Fully Illustrated Guide*. Buffalo, N.Y.: Amherst Media, Inc., 1997.

Tydings, Kenneth S. *The Canon Guide to 35mm Photography*. New York: Greenberg, 1954.

White, Robert. *Discovering Cameras, 1945-65*. Buckinghamshire, U.K.: Shire Publications, Ltd., 1995.

Williamson, David. *Comprehensive Guide for Camera Collectors*. Atlen, PA: Schiffer, 2004.

Canon Instructions and Product Guides

It is still possible to acquire relatively complete sets of instructions, product guides, and other documents. Originals are often sold with cameras and other items while many are sold separately. In additon, both reprints and digital copies are available from a variety of sources.

In spite of their general availability, its occasionally challenging to find specific items. I've come to rely on a handful of sources:

http://web.archive.org/web/20060318003234/canonfd.com/choose.htm

http://www.paradesquare.ca/canon_fd/

http://www.lensinc.net/freeuser.html

http://www.butkus.org/chinon/canon.htm

http://www.craigcamera.com

Users Groups and Forums

http://tech.groups.yahoo.com/group/CanonFD/

http://photo.net/canon-fd-camera-forum/

http://www.adaptall-2.org/ tamron

http://groups.yahoo.com/group/Kiron-Klub/

http://tech.groups.yahoo.com/group/camera-fix/

Other Internet Sites

Christian Rollinger's Canon FD Documentation Project is archived at http://classic-web.archive.org/web/20071029091648/www.canonfd.com/choose.htm

http://cybernetdenis.net/3rdparty.htm

http://www.jollinger.com/photo/meters/meters/canon_fp.html with pic

http://www.thecamerasite.net/01_SLR_Cameras/Pages/canon-SLR.htm#fp

http://www.cameraquest.com/index.html

http://www.mir.com.my/rb/photography/

http://www.photographyhistory.com/idcclist.html

http://betezra.tripod.com/lightmeters

http://www.adaptall-2.org/

http://captjack.exaktaphile.com/canonflex/Canonflex.htm

http://www.edsawyer.com/lenstests/

http://www.fdreview.com/

http://throughavintagelens.com/2010/04/restoring-vintage-cameras-i-the-golden-rule-an-ebay-buying-guide/

http://throughavintagelens.com/2010/04/restoring-vintage-cameras-ii-tools/